The Some
and Noth

DEATH

A Book To Read
Before You Die

Will Parfitt

By The Same Author

KABBALAH

The Living Qabalah
The Elements of the Qabalah
The New Living Qabalah
The Complete Guide to the Kabbalah
Kabbalah for Life

PSYCHOLOGY

Walking Through Walls
The Elements of Psychosynthesis
Psychosynthesis: The Elements and Beyond

POETRY

Through The Gates of Matter

The Something
and Nothing of
DEATH

A Book To Read
Before You Die

Will Parfitt

PS AVALON

Glastonbury, England

© Will Parfitt 2008

First published in the U.K. in 2008 by PS Avalon

PS Avalon
Box 1865, Glastonbury
Somerset, BA6 8YR, U.K.
www.psavalon.com

Design: Will Parfitt

ISBN 978-0-9552786-4-8

Contents

*

dedicated to

Helen Yates

*"To live is to die a thousand deaths,
but there is only one fire, one eternity."*

Normandi Ellis

✳

INTRODUCTION

Monk to Zen Master: What happens after death, master?
Zen master: I don't know.
Monk: But you are a master!
Master: Yes, but I'm not a dead one yet. [1]

After you die there is either something or nothing. All the possibilities – all the beliefs, fantasies, fears, imaginings and so on – of what happens to us after we die are something rather than nothing. If there really is *something*, won't it be amazing to find out what it is. On the other hand, if there is *nothing* then, by definition, you won't be there to experience it, so you won't know anything about it anyway.

That the something after death could be terrible – hell, for instance – is quite a thought. Imagine the pain in burning forever. No, don't imagine it, it's too terrible. We would prefer this something to be wonderful – a personalised heaven, for instance, designed exactly as we would want it to be, or reincarnation a step on from our current state. Yet perhaps it is better not to make this something after death into either wonderful or terrible, because then we are placing a human dual view onto something – the after-life – that is beyond duality. In any case, if there *is* something, just think: you are dead and experiencing it. There is an after-life after all!

What of nothing, the experience of which is one of our deepest existential fears? The abyss, the chasm of 'nothingness', the bottomless pit where we lose all sense of identity, where we don't *become* as nothing, we *are* nothing. From the limited perspective of life it is most certainly awful. But think about it: you won't be thinking about it. As the poet Andrew Marvell commented: "The grave's a fine and private place, But none I think do there embrace." [2]

Something or nothing? Some religions could be accused of trying to make something out of nothing. Others work hard at proving there is nothing but nothing. Either way, like all of us, they can only enter the human condition most fully by accepting that we do not know, and we will not know until we die. Like the Zen Master, we aren't dead yet. This book explores some of the possibilities in nothing *and* something and the probability that after we die there will be something or there will be nothing. Either way there is nothing now to stop us exploring and enjoying the journey towards our ultimate life experience... death.

∗

The vast majority of people who have ever lived have believed in reincarnation and the vast majority still do.[3] If reincarnation is true, then it might be interesting to reincarnate as a tree or an eagle or a genius. Most beliefs involving reincarnation don't give you a choice, however, except in through living a 'good' life (good defined by the precepts of each particular belief system), so increasing your odds of, if not a chosen then at least an improved lot (spiritually even if not necessarily materially.)

Almost as many people believe that after dying they might enter some kind of heaven or hell.[4] If this is true, then it would clearly be better to go to heaven than to hell; it might be boring but at least it would be safe. But for eternity even heaven might become a little too familiar. Over the centuries the idea of going to hell has terrified millions and millions of people. To not be terrified by the idea of eternal fire and torture would not be real. It seems to me equally unreal to imagine a loving god who would inflict something so awful upon anyone (even our worst enemies deserve better than that, don't they?)

The other most widely adopted possibility for what happens after death is that we merge with the creator or godhead, back into the universal oneness.[5] If this is true then the most pleasure would come with the merging, assuming that we are still experiencing similar desires as in life. Once we have merged with the creator or the universe, there isn't anything left to do or, by implication, to experience, except the one thing – the bliss of oneness. There's nothing awful about this, of course, but it does have some of the disadvantages of an eternal heaven.

The last great optional belief about what happens to us after we die is that nothing does; there is nothing after death at all, nothing to experience and no 'us' to experience it. If there isn't any you to experience it then there is certainly nothing to be frightened of and indeed, the oblivion option does mean freedom from all the pains of life, including any illnesses and disabilities that preceded death. True, but as we cannot by definition experience this option, even if it is the truth, it seems to me more interesting to explore the possibilities, and hold to a choice to believe that, whatever it is, there will be something. It is probably best, though, along the way towards death, that we don't cling onto any of the possibilities of what might happen after death. It may just surprise us![6]

To face death confers inner strength for it brings us more authentically into the fullness of our lives; in other words, it brings us closer to freedom. Living wisely is to prepare for dying well, not for some promise of what will happen after death but because living wisely brings its own merit. There is nothing to avoid, nothing to be attached to except the moment as it is. Just as we generate new cells in our bodies each day[7], in a constant process of regeneration and renewal, so collectively we are engaged in a vast and ecstatic recycling of energy. Everything changes and nothing is ever lost. Thus truly the whole is, always has been and always will be, greater than the sum of its parts. That is equally true before and after death. All particles have relative immortality and the limited lifetime of any particular combination of particles is something to be celebrated not feared. Living your life now, surrendering to what is, confers meaning on life *and* death through transcending all concerns about their difference. As we cannot have one without the other, life and death, twin poles of our experience, are not nor ever have been separate.

How To Use This Book

If you flick through the pages of *The Something and Nothing of Death* you'll see it is mostly composed of short, easy-to-digest sections that make it easy for you to dip in and out as you wish. You can, of course, also start at the beginning of the book and read straight through to the end where you will find quite a few pages of fairly lengthy notes. These are referenced throughout the main text but also can be read in their own right.

When you meet the term '*reflection*' in this book it indicates that the following section, whilst it may simply be read, can also be used as an exercise in mindful self-inquiry. Before all 'reflections' spend a few moments relaxing and centering yourself, ensuring you have enough time to complete the section without being disturbed. Take as long as you need to go through the suggestions as it is always better with such inner work to go slowly rather than rushing. If you are someone who doesn't do exercises in books, then at least read them so you know what they are suggesting. For many people, simply reading through an exercise has a powerful effect.

Finally, taking a light approach to reading this book, and then in small portions, may help you connect with and keep a perspective on what can be a deeply moving topic.

✳

PART 1

LIFE

"Die, my dear?
Why that's the last thing I'll do!"

Groucho Marx [8]

Death In Life

An awareness of the presence of death is always with us during our lives but we never know when we are to die – it could be this very moment, now as you are reading or I am writing these words. How do we deal with that? What is it like to be aware of death in life? What is it like to not be aware of death in life? Is it better to be aware of death's presence or not?

The deepest inquiry leads us to what meaning death has for the living; what it means for us, whilst still alive, to be aware of the presence of death. On a more speculative level, perhaps paradoxically, we will also explore if life has meaning for the dead. If something – anything – does come after death, it may be that how we interact with death whilst still alive profoundly affects our after-death experience.

As a day never goes by in my life when I don't think about death, I find it rather strange to imagine that some people may spend little or no time thinking about death. But in any case, underneath conscious thoughts, behind the level where we may think about it or not, death has a deep underlying presence that affects us in all our actions, in everything we do in our lives. It is important we accept the place of death in life and, in fact, many ancient traditions[9] stress such an understanding is powerful not as a source of terror but as an agent for freedom. Death may even be seen as a friend or ally whose presence supports and teaches us rather than frightening us.

Death is intrinsically bound up with life. Life and death are twin poles of the same thing, and in being so reflect other rhythmic aspects of nature – the phases of the moon, the sun rising and setting, the ebb and flow of tides, the cycle of the seasons, and so on. Just as night follows day and day follows night, then it may be a primitive logic but it is not really so strange to believe that if death follows life it must also mean that life follows death. Everything passes away, true, but don't we experience in this life that, equally, things come back round?

Spring is not a one-off event; it arrives each year, then passes and, at the appropriate time, it comes back again. Maybe they're all just kidding themselves, but more people by far believe this one life isn't everything, and whilst there is no scientific proof of this, there is an abundance of anecdotal evidence backed up by a wealth of feeling. And as no one can be completely sure as to whether or not anything exists after death, it may even be the case that you experience after death exactly what you believed you would experience. That's a salutary thought, especially if believing there will be nothing means there will be nothing.

Throughout human history there have been innumerable different ideas as to what else there might be beyond life and what death means for us. If there is something other than nothing, we don't seem to be able to get a fix on what it might be. In one way or another, though, such belief involves conceptualising death as neither an annihilation nor a release, ideas that are acceptable to existentialists and humanists, but rather as a rebirth, regeneration or some kind of resurrection. Death may be seen, for instance, as a door to a new round of existence, perhaps even in a physical sense; as a transition to becoming another human being; as a greater or lesser being than you are now, anything from an intergalactic intelligence to a humble earthworm; an entrance to some kind of paradise or some form of hell, where you party or suffer depending upon your life actions; and so on. If it is the case that after death you experience exactly what you believed you would experience, there may be things imagined, an eternal hell, for example, that are worse than if there is nothing.

Perhaps after death there is something that we cannot possibly imagine whatsoever, and as nobody has ever come back to tell us what is on the other side of death there is no way we will ever be able to imagine it. Actually, there are some people who claim to have returned from death to describe their experience[10], but just because that is their experience, assuming you believe it, that does not prove it will be the same for you when you die.

Plato said our living is a preparation for our dying.[11] We could interpret that to mean that we should in some way use our lives to prepare for death. Alternatively we can take it to mean that everything we do in our lives is, in one way or another, a part of such preparation. Each moment that we are alive, as we come into that moment, contains everything that we are, the totality of our existence. I can't be alive in the past and I'm certainly not alive yet in the future, so all I can be is really present in this moment. Yet it does not always seem to be so: sometimes we're very un-present to ourselves and either we miss the splendour and beauty of life or we inadvertently get ourselves caught into things with which we would do better not to get involved. We all have experienced how doing things unconsciously leads to results other than what we want. If we apply this knowledge to our dying, it suggests we would do well to remember that death may be present in each moment. If we live life in the present, aware that life is a preparation for dying, then in dying we cannot miss the powerful and potentially liberating experience that death will be. We then do not retreat into fantasies that lead us nowhere, but remain present with the beauty of existence in life and, when it comes, death.

Some traditions take this idea to a deeper level, where the life that follows death is seen as a continuation of the impulses and character traits formed before death, which is what then leads to us to reincarnate in a form appropriate to how we have lived in this life.[12] The idea is that as we advance in our engagement with life, and inevitably with death too, we can learn to live in a way that ensures we will incarnate each time in a successively better form. We can then grow more independent of the mechanical rebirth process and walk a new path towards spiritual freedom. For death not to be followed by rebirth would mean you'd lived a perfect life according to the principles of your faith. This basically comes down to saying that living wisely is the best preparation for dying. Whether death is a one off experience or might be one of many deaths in a series of lives, whether we see our life as a preparation for dying or more specifically for dying well, it behoves us to pay attention to the presence of death now, before it is too late.

✳

Facing the Unavoidable

Death often does not seem to be friendly, in fact quite the opposite. To truly encompass death we must include the other side where death is a destroyer, a bringer of pain, the one who takes our loved ones away, that comes with chaos and catastrophe, that is associated with the slaughter of war, and so on. This version of death isn't something we can think about and reflect on but instead something that smashes into our emotions in painful and shocking ways. This death is one of sadness and pain where our emotions literally overwhelm us with grief, sorrow, pain or anger (and sometimes even joy.) Death is then not like a computer game where you might be given three lives. This death is truly a destroyer, the destroyer of life.

Jean Paul Sartre called death 'the terminator'[13] but unlike in the movies there cannot be a sequel, the door closes, and your whole existence, everything you've been is now in the past. This is true in each moment, so in that sense in each moment we also die. Whatever death touches becomes fully impervious to human action, according to Sartre. We cannot change what is already dead and we don't have the power to bring life to non-living substances, although some aspects of modern scientific research lead us to think that might not always be so. Realistically, our technology is more focussed on how we can prolong life thus supporting the kind of life that pretends death isn't part of it.

Some people rail at the idea of prolonging life, really wanting the release that death can bring, not necessarily because they are in pain from some disease, or have cancer, but simply because they believe that life has its limits. Whatever we think about or try to understand about life and death, there is no doubt death has a connection to suffering and the painful side of human existence. We are only too sharply brought up against this in the modern news media which can show us many aspects of death from, for instance, the painful death of a disgraced dictator to the murder of children in an unwanted war.

*

Identity and Soul

Some of the particles inside our bodies might have originated in a distant star,[14] and any particle within us has relative immortality. If my body slowly decomposes after I die, then all the little particles (atoms and so on) that make me up go off into space. At some point they might possibly join with other particles, other atoms and so on, and become something else; in fact if we wait long enough that may even be inevitable. But even if they do not join with others they are not going to die, they are not going to be anywhere else but floating around in space as long as space exists, which is meaningless as a measure. If right now I consider all the particles, all the atoms and electrons and so on that make me up, everything that makes up what I call 'myself', that makes up 'Will' right now, this particular singular combination of particles most certainly has a strictly limited lifetime. If I don't hold an attachment to the particular combination of particles I now am, however, but allow myself to melt or merge into the particles that make me up, each of these particles having their relative immortality means that even though the composite 'me' may not exist beyond my death, the parts of me will do, and relatively forever.

That brings up a question about identity. If we believe that the sum is greater than the whole of the parts, such as a painting, for instance, being more than the paint and canvas, is my identity greater than the sum of its parts? Take water as an example; water has different properties than its constituents – water is made of up hydrogen and oxygen both of which are invisible gases which have their own particular properties. There is no way if you look at water, dive in it, drink it, or do anything else with it, that you would necessarily deduce any connection between water and its component elements. In the ordinary physical and sensory world we inhabit, the properties of the components of water do not tell us anything about the properties of water itself. If we apply this to human identity and all these little particles that make me up, with their relative immortality, then it appears that I am something more than them. Just as water is more than its component elements, I am something more than the parts that make me up. This is the soul, or 'spiritual intelligence' of some kind, that this reasoning leads us to believe must exist within us. This 'soul', regulating all the activities going on in my body, as well as directing and interacting with all my feeling and thinking processes, most of which I am never conscious of, may actually survive the death of the body. Perhaps there is a soul that also has relative immortality, which has nothing to do with the parts of me but is a whole that comes from the sum of the parts.[15] If there is such a thing, perhaps it survives the death of the body – indeed, it can seem stranger to think of it not doing so.

It is more helpful not to think of soul in that way, as something eternal, or a given, but rather to think of soul as a potential that awakens if we choose to activate it. One of the ways to activate it is to reflect deeply, and continuously, on the place of death in our life. Once we start reflecting on and being mindful of the processes of death, it brings us to life, it supports the growth of soul within us. One of the deepest and most meaningful processes we can be aware of in life is this ever-present death. The more we allow that awareness, instead of seeing life and death as two separate sides of a polarity –I'm either alive or I'm dead – we move to a place where I have both life and death. Being aware of and acknowledging the dead part of me brings a greater sense of wholeness to the live part of me, the very process that can activate the potential of soul.

*

The Journey of Life

L ife can be understood as a journey or cycle of individuation[16], meaning that as we move through life we become more true to ourselves. Looked at this way, we can glean a sense of the whole process of development and evolution from exploring the journey of our own individual life. The journey each of us takes through life can be seen, at least metaphorically and perhaps literally, as the journey of the soul coming into incarnation. What happens to each of us, from when we are born to when we die then has meaning beyond the specific content of the events of that particular life. The whole of our lives is greater than the sum of its parts. We may discover, for instance, that we are not just personalities but something else runs through our lives, a deeper presence or knowing. This 'something' that brings meaning to the journey of life inevitably has to include all the difficult and dark bits as well the light and bright bits for it to be complete.

Reflection [17]

Reflect on your life for a while now, becoming aware of your life as a journey from conception, through birth, to death. Spend a while simply reflecting on this journey you are taking, including a realistic consideration of where you are on that journey right now.

Look at the following line that represents your lifetime from your birth until your death:

B -- D

Being as honest with yourself as you are willing to be, consider how far along that line you believe you are. You might like to put a cross on the line to represent this. Spend some time reflecting on this, noting any thoughts, feelings and sensations that may arise from such contemplation.

Now reflect how on your journey of life, you make many smaller journeys (for instance the journey of school, of marriage, of parenthood, of work, and so on.) Also consider how within any and all of those smaller journeys, you make even smaller ones (such as the journey of reading this book, the journey to brush your teeth you make each day, and so on…)

Connect now particularly to the journey of reading this book. At this point in your journey, what are you feeling? What are you feeling and what do you think about being on this journey? Don't start thinking about this book, stay reflecting on what you think and feel about the journey you have taken in order to read it.

What thoughts are you having right now? Do not censor or judge anything that comes to mind, simply observe the flow of thoughts that come in and out of your awareness. Spend some little while with this reflection.

Now shift your awareness to your body – what does your body feel about being wherever you are at this very moment? What sensations are you experiencing? What does your body have to say to you right now? (Do you need to move your physical position – if so, do so.)

Now consider the journey that you undertook to get to this very moment so far today from when you awoke this morning – waking up, dressing and so on, people you might have made contact with – partners, children, friends, neighbours, whatever else you have done so far today, including what feelings, thoughts and sensations you have been experiencing.

Now tune into and reflect once more on your whole life journey, not only the everyday events, but also the sense of being on a deeper life journey.

Consider: where are you on your life journey? Are you coasting, passing through a transition, ready for a change? Are you more engaged with the old or the new in your life? Do you feel awake and tuned in, or perhaps do you feel more distant or absent? Don't make judgments on your responses, simply observe how you respond.

Be aware of whatever it is in your life that has brought you to this very moment (of course not all of which will be conscious, but focus on what you do know.)

What are you here on your life journey for? What is your sense of your purpose for being alive? Trust what responses come, even if you do not understand them. (If you are keeping a journal this might be a good time to note down your responses to this exercise.)

Whatever has brought you here, you are undoubtedly here now – you can't be anywhere else but where you are at the very moment you read this. Affirm strongly to yourself the rightness to be you, here right now.

✳

Between Birth and Death

In life we don't always feel like we are in the right place at the right time. Any unavoidable event we don't want to face, such as a difficult appointment, job deadline or personal confrontation usually brings with it emotions such as anxiety, dread and fear. These are feelings that can be totally overwhelming and yet they involve situations in our lives which we know are temporary. What then of death which is permanent and universal? Instead of giving us a chance of looking at our lives more objectively and bringing us into the present moment, the anxious feelings associated with the presence of death may actually be negatively overwhelming, dispiriting and bring a sense of doom.

At the deepest levels within us there appears to be nothing other than complete and utter silence. Our consciousness may then simply be a way of overlaying and attempting to avoid the presence of death, but can equally be an attempt to bring us face to face with death, thus strengthening us and bringing us more authentically into the present moment. To be truly in our lives means seeing death as a phase of life, not as an ending but as a new beginning from whence we renew our search for understanding. So rather than denying death or allowing ourselves to be overwhelmed by its presence, we may do better to acknowledge it and consult it as an ally. Death then helps us to remember that each experience we have, whether mental, emotional or physical lasts for a limited time.

However intense an experience is whilst it lasts, once it is over it inevitably fades, even those experiences which at the time are so vivid we think we'll never forget them. Although at a cellular or physical level we may have deep memories of our birth, we don't consciously remember, it has passed. Whilst it is possible under certain uncommon circumstances that we may be able to remember our birth, we certainly cannot remember our death which has not yet happened. Birth, ageing and dying, like all other events, can only be experienced in the present. I may even remember my birth well (however unlikely that may seem) but I can no longer *experience* it for it is in the past. Similarly, it is clear that I cannot experience my dying in the future. I'll experience death when it happens, not before.

Our ongoing experience is the gap between birth and death – life – during which time we are ageing, but even then I can't experience my ageing from last week, I can only experience myself ageing now. All experience is in the now. Mindfulness is helpful, to realise that, whatever experience we are having, we can be attentive and receptive to the experience.[18] This enables us to become more attentive to the process of the life we are living. We may awaken and thus avoid unthinking repetition. The notion of being awake in life seems very positive: no one wants to go through their life even half asleep, or even half dead – but what about being awake at the time of death? If we are to awaken in our lives this inevitably means we have to be awake at our death. It may seem rather positive and relatively easy if we wish to die peacefully in our sleep, but when we reflect on it we may realise it is much better to be able to die peacefully whilst awake.

However we bandy words about and consider death as a transition or as part of life, in a very clear sense it marks the end of a life. When you are dead, whatever might be afterwards, you will no longer be the 'you' that you were before death. One individual dying out of six billion or so planetary inhabitants may seem insignificant or unimportant, but for the person who has died their death is the most significant thing that has happened in their lives, whether they have any awareness of it or not. At a collective level, however, an individual death may also not be so insignificant. Each death inevitably involves a recycling of energy and material, and this is a necessary principle of life. If nothing was ever recycled the biosphere would get fuller and fuller up, our planet would be even busier than it already appears to be, and eventually there wouldn't be enough room for everyone and everything.

※

Youth and Age

Whilst on the one hand the death of child or young adult is considered unjust or unfair and brings with it difficult emotional responses, many people come to view the elderly as having lived out their lives, and the death of a person being a natural and inevitable event that follows a gradual process of decay and degeneration. The ancient riddle of the Sphinx shows how old this pattern of belief is: the Sphinx asks, 'what is it that has one voice but becomes four footed, two footed and finally three footed?' Oedipus is able to offer the correct answer to the Sphinx – the human being who crawls on all fours when an infant, walks on two legs when an adult, and then leans on a walking stick when aged.[19]

Thomas Hanna[20], the founder of Somatics, uses this myth to illustrate that how we approach aging (and by implication, death) is largely affected by our belief systems and expectations. He sees expectation as a self fulfilling process, being not only a prediction of the future but a direct contributor to making it happen. What we expect to happen does happen. If we take body discomforts as a sign of serious disease and breakdown as we would expect in older age then we are giving in to a presumed fatality. As Hanna puts it so succinctly: 'To anticipate pathology is, functionally, tantamount to intending it.'

If we look into the etymology of the word 'age' we find it merely means a period of existence and, more importantly, what characterises this period. We are led to realise that 'to age' or 'to grow old' means either to grow, increase and become taller and deeper or to decrease, decay, wear out, become decrepit and useless. The direction of human aging is therefore not fixed but open, and dependent largely upon what we believe and expect as we approach and enter into this phase of the journey of life.

To quote Hanna once more, he states quite bluntly: 'To despise the fact of aging is not only to despise life but to betray a pitiful ignorance of the nature of life.'[21] In our modern, topsy-turvy world, we tend to at best ignore and at worst despise the aging process (and the aged) whilst at the same time adulating youth. Yet surely youth is a stage of life to be put behind us as we grow taller and deeper (thus fulfilling the yearning of youth by transcending it rather than clinging on to it after its sell-by date.) Rather than worshipping at the temple of a false and superficial image of youthfulness we can take charge of our lives, never more importantly than when approaching death, and enjoy the filling out that age brings however few or many years we have already lived.

If we compare some of the qualities of youth and age we can find some interesting differences:

• youth has strength, age has skill;
• youth has speed, age has efficiency;
• youth is quick, age is deliberate;
• youth has energy, age has judgement;
• youth is a stage of innocence, age of wisdom;
• youth is emptiness awaiting fullness, age is fullness manifest;
• youth has the beauty of newness, age has the beauty of achievement;
• youth has the glow of promise, age has radiance of accomplishment;
• youth is a time of seeding and cultivation, age a time of fruiting and harvest.

The real essence of youth is to be growing, to be looking forward to the promise of happiness and fulfilment that becoming an adult entails. If we can keep to this attitude right through life, an attitude of positive expectation, of expecting the best from life, then we age not only gracefully but also wisely. We can measure our achievements in skill, efficiency, deliberation, and wise judgement with pride, and face the adventure of death as an inevitable and meaningful component of a full growth-led life. We can expect a good death for this is our birth-right. Whilst we may have lost our connection to this during our earlier years, we can now embrace it with open arms and an open heart.

✳

Being An Elder

The last two turns of the wheel on the journey of life are the change from being a mature adult into an elder, then the final one from being an elder into death. Of course, not everyone (either developmentally or literally!) reaches the status of 'elder', but with certainty everyone reaches death. On reflection, it seems that one of the major features of a life that can confer the status of 'elder' on someone is not what age they reach (although they may well deserve the title for just for having reached a certain age) but how well they have integrated the lessons of life. This is not to say anyone is better or worse than another, just that we all live unique and idiosyncratic lives, developing more in some areas and less in others. Perhaps the truest sign of integration – and the wisdom that comes with it – is recognising that we are just right as we are, wherever and however we have developed through life. Certainly the wisest old people I have met exhibit great acceptance of themselves and others.

Before continuing, spend a little while reflecting on wisdom and what in your experience makes a person wise. Consider what you fear most about getting older and what you look forward to as you get older.

Reflection

Whatever your actual physical age is, reflect on how old you are and how old you feel. Are they the same age? For many not so – people are often saying how they feel older or younger than they actually are and the fashion industry (and our wider society) encourage people to attempt to look younger. Strange in a way that we don't have face creams to make us look wiser!

How old did you feel ten years ago – older, younger or the same as now?

How old did you feel when you were in your late teens?

Reflect back on your childhood: - what was your skin like then? how did it feel to touch your skin?

Feel your own skin now – touch your hands, face, any other exposed areas of your skin – how is it different from when you were a child?

What feelings, or other responses and reactions do you have to doing to this?

Imagine you are the child you were, standing before a mirror... see your hair, eyes, face in your imagination...

Now look in a mirror – look at yourself now – look at your hair, your eyes, and your face – what difference has aging made to your appearance?

What difference is there in your own response to your appearance, now as compared to back then?
How do you feel about your appearance now?

Consider your whole body now. How has it changed since you were younger? What changes has your body gone through?...

What changes have there been in your feelings about life, and feelings about yourself?

What changes have there been in your ideas about life, and ideas about yourself?

What about your ideas about ageing? What has changed in your responses to ageing since you were younger?

How do you feel, now you are ageing and know it?

*

Life Span

There are six billion or so humans[22] on this planet and all of us, at whatever age we die, will die within our lifetime. Does that seem too obvious? Read it again, carefully: all of us, all six billion humans on this planet, in fact all living creatures alive on this planet, will – must – die within their own lifetime. As everyone dies, you cannot have a life without death and your life must include your death.

Of the six billion or so people alive, one hundred million or so die each year. We know of specific deaths – my mother died, my uncle died, my friend died, and so on – and we have no choice but to be aware of these specific deaths. As a rule, though, we usually ignore the mass annual death of our fellow humans. Yet it is quite striking if we bring it back to our awareness: that not 'somebody out there' but 'somebody right here' will die, not a hundred million of 'them' but rather a hundred million of us die each year.

We also know that a greater or lesser number than this of babies are born each year.[23] If we include both ends of life, birth and death, then on our collective journey through life, we see that as some people die others are born. There is, as it were, a constant replacement and renewal, a re-cycling of life. This recycling process is necessary for it connects us into the larger process of life. We can learn that our life is not something eternal but is part of a cyclical pattern that everything that comes alive is a trade off for something that dies, that whilst we may change in form, in essence we are always part of one constantly changing process.

Now reflect on the average life span of the following animals:

a mayfly: *24 hours*
a firefly: *2 months*
a garden slug: *3 years*
a fox: *10 years*

a cow: *22 years*
a pigeon: *26 years*
a starfish: *35 years*
a donkey: *45 years*
 an elephant: *70 years*
a human: around *80 years*
a land tortoise: *200 years.* [24]

    As far as we know everything dies and we can easily surmise even the most long–living things, whatever they might be, will eventually die. But as far as we know human beings are the only creatures that think about and imagine their own deaths. Although many will deny it, most people have at least some fear of death and try to avoid thinking about it, despite the fact that underneath any protestations otherwise, this fear plays an important role in influencing behaviour. It is not surprising with such a fear of death that most people try to avoid it.

    Fritz Perls[25], founder of Gestalt Therapy, commented:

    'It is obvious that an eagle's potential will be actualized in roaming the sky, diving down on smaller animals for food, and in building nests.

    'It is obvious that an elephants potential will be actualized in size, power and clumsiness.

    'No eagle will want to be an elephant; no elephant to be eagle ... how absurd it would be if they, like humans, had fantasies, dissatisfactions, and self-deceptions...

    'Leave this to the human – to try to be something he is not, to have ideals that cannot be reached, to be cursed with perfectionism so as to be safe from criticism, and to open the road to unending mental torture.'

Is there really anything to fear in death? Why do we humans fear something that for an eagle or elephant is simply part of the process of life?

✳

Walking with Death

Death is not just about dying; through accepting our initial responses of fear and avoidance to even the idea of death, we may experience death as a liberating force, a freeing from outworn and constricting patterns that have been encumbering and stifling us.

Death is always with us – we can imagine it is just over our left shoulder, waiting to tap us when our time is up; or just half a breath away, we never know when it will call us. It is vital to acknowledge this presence and start to build relationship with death.

Reflection

Before continuing make sure you have plenty of time for the following activity and for being with what it brings up for you. Read it through quite lightly at first before delving into its suggestions and only go as far as you feel safe to do so, trusting your own inner sense of what is right for you.

Imagine yourself at the centre of a circle, breathe slowly and regularly, then either imagine yourself or actually step onto and then walk round the circumference of your circle clockwise, all the while silently reflecting as you walk.

Walk round this circle, projecting death into the middle of the circle. Put everything you think, feel, sense and fear about death into the circle whose circumference you are walking.

As you keep walking: consider the people in your life who have died ... simply allow yourself to reflect on these people and notice how this makes you feel in your body ... and what emotions come up? Associated thoughts ... allow them to be present right now...

Now as you keep walking: consider the times in your life when you have faced your own death... illnesses, accidents, depressions ... allow yourself to be aware of the associated sensations, feelings, thoughts...

Keep walking and imagine you are on your own deathbed.

Reflect now on the different ways you can die – peacefully, of old age, in a road accident, younger than expected, with cancer, aids, from heart failure, from gradual decay, with others, alone in a flat with no one knowing, surrounded by your family, alone in hospital, in an airplane, at sea ...

Still walking, consider now, if you had just died, how your corpse might be:

Reflect on your corpse, lifeless and bloodless ... the skeleton, the bones of your corpse ... the flesh, eaten by bacteria, fungi and insects ... reflect on the gruesomeness of the situation ... now consider silence ... consider death ... [26]

Keep walking: project all of your thoughts, fantasies, feelings, reactions, sensations, responses to death into the circle...

Now stop walking, turn and face into this circle of death:
– from where you are now, taking your time to sense and feel this journey as you experience it, walk into the territory of death and surrender to its influence...

– once inside, begin to develop a relationship with death

– locate in your body your contact point with death

– where in you is your response to death

– allow yourself to experience and express this now as much as you are willing

– face up to and, if it feels right for you, dialogue with death

When you are ready, return to your original place on the circumference of the circle.

Turn and acknowledge the presence of death outside you and once more within the circle.

Thoroughly close your circle, bringing yourself back to the sacred space of your own life and situation. Spend time reflecting on what you discovered about your relationship with death.

✳

The Fool's Journey

Ego develops as a container for all our energies, to protect and support us through our lives. We should not denigrate our relationship with ego. Ego is not a good master but is an excellent friend. When we become totally identified with ego (a stage we all go through, and which people do not necessarily pass beyond) we live by our learned and adapted behaviour patterns which are based on a split between oneself, other people and the outer world, predicated upon the mechanisms of what was once a useful container but has now become a limiting prison. We have built ego to protect us and now our unfulfilled needs control us. This is sometimes called the adapted personality. It does not have to be a permanent condition.

The ancient system of tarot[27], if seen as more than just cards for fortune telling, in some hands a rather dubious activity, but instead as a pictorial representation of our life journey, offers interesting insights into the journey of life and our developmental stages, can be used as a potent guide to self-development and for the realisation of creative potential. The tarot is a way of framing, articulating and evoking these energies we experience and express through our life journey into conscious recognition.

Each tarot card represents a facet of who you are. The first two cards in a tarot deck are the Fool and the Magus. On the surface the Fool is stupid, often depicted as blindly stepping over a cliff. Similarly the Magus is wise, conjuring the world into existence through magical arts. On a deeper level, however, we find the Fool is not as first appears; letting go into the world, surrendering to a larger wisdom, he or she lives life to the full. The Fool that persists in folly becomes wise. And the Magus is not so wise when fixated with ideas and techniques and missing the natural flow of energy, trying to make things happen that will happen anyway in their own good time. We have to discover how to trust our inner processes both when we feel 'wise' and when we feel 'foolish'. Accepting ourselves as we are, we recognize where we are in life and can creatively and joyously divine our future.

The only certainty in our lives is that everything changes, but our lives are not predetermined by outside forces, we really can make choices. Life is the search for and discovery of self, experienced through a constant polarity between moving forwards towards death and / or backwards towards the womb[28]. At all stages we become attached to our experiences and it is necessary for us to engage with these experiences and learn to differentiate. We forget; so, conversely, we are offered the opportunity to remember. To re-member is to put ourselves back together through an act of disidentification that enables a move towards union with consciousness and choice.

Moments of crisis force an awakening in the journey of life, or sometimes we have moments of spontaneous awakening, but however they arise, we can realise at these times of awakening that we are on an adventure, a quest for determination and courage as old as humanity itself, the challenge of knowing oneself. The three tarot cards most associated with times of transition are called the Wheel of Fortune (fairly self-evident), the Devil and Death. What these cards represent is worth contemplating even if you do not have any particular interest in the tarot as they offer a universal understanding beyond anything to do with the cards.

The Wheel of Fortune can be taken to represent life transitions, times of awakening and crisis (such as at mid life.) Thrust onto the Wheel of Fortune, we separate from our past experiences and knowledge which is no longer sufficient to guide us through life. Our parents or guardians, our teachers, even our sense of self, our ego, are no longer able to protect us in our interactions with the world. We find ourselves entering darkness, confronting our carefully constructed ego-self with the depths of our own psyche. We are forced to adjust to a new life, a new way of being, possibly to sacrifice our old values, no longer with the optimism of youth but with the reality of maturity. We pass beyond life as it has been known and the Wheel of Fortune forces us to re-appraise ourselves, to find our own inner star to guide us through what is sometimes called the dark night of the soul, facing all the terrors such times of transition can throw at us, including what in the tarot is represented by the Devil.

Sometimes the Devil is associated with the afterlife though there is an alternative view that the Devil is more concerned with life than what happens after it. Still, there is the threat that we might go to hell after we die if we don't live well enough. The ruler of this hell is the Devil, this horned, fiery evil character who will ensure you are tortured for eternity because of your bad deeds. What a threat; if it were true and we knew it to be certain, then it would certainly change how we live. Doubt that? Then consider the Islamist terrorist who willingly blows himself up because he 'knows for certain' he will enter paradise. Of course, we know no such thing – and, interestingly, people are much keener to not believe in a Devil in the after-life than they are of a benign god. After all, when we die, if we experience anything, it is natural to want it to be pleasant. Just don't be manipulated into believing that you have to live by someone else's rules to ensure you don't go to hell or will go to heaven.

What of this Devil in life? The Devil is only evil in so far as we have been conditioned to be fearful of the life force itself. The energy of life can be intoxicating, primal and raw; it can be dangerous, but it is a far less dangerous than fearfully holding ourselves back from living life to the full. The Devil cuts through convention and traditional morality to create a space for creativity to blossom. To build a relationship with the energies represented by the Devil is to break down old structures, to laugh, play and celebrate the dance of life.

The Devil represents, individually and collectively, what we repress (positive and negative things) and what we fear: fear itself, anger, sadness, shame/guilt, and positive energy such as joy, and fully expressing who we are. To connect with and to stop fearing the Devil is to let go to these feelings, thoughts, sensations and just be alive – simply said but much more difficult to do.

Reflection

Reflect on your feelings about being yourself in your life: what do you fear if you connect to life energy in an unbridled way?

What is it like for you to be angry, to allow angry energy to well up without constraint?

How do you cope with loss, sadness, grief – what is it like to allow these energies without restraint?

What would it be like if you had no shame or guilt – how would you be?

What about joy and happiness – what is it in you that holds back from fully expressing your positive feelings – what reserve is there, what would it be like to allow yourself to be filled with joy?

It is not only the devil who is pictured as fearsome. Death has been oft represented in a gruesome and fearful manner, no less so than in tarot cards where death is a scythe wielding skeleton that chops people down, sometimes in the prime of their life, sometimes even as children, or even new-born babes.[29] Death's scythe is relentless and, apparently, impartial – if you get in its way, you are a goner. In the tarot, the card entitled Death is usually said to also imply rebirth; this is true for a Tarot interpretation but the force, the energy depicted by the card is what it says it is: death.

Death is seen in the tarot as an essential stage in the journey of individuation. The major cards of a tarot deck depict the journey from the new born, pure innocent egoless child represented by the Fool to the fulfilment of life in the outer world, depicted by the last card the 'Universe' or 'World'. The twenty cards in-between are ascribed to different stages on our life journey; the first third or so of the cards representing childhood development; the middle third representing separation and liminality, the necessary stage for change and development to not only occur but to be established; and the final third or so depicting the return from transitional phases with the new grounded and mature condition. Interestingly the middle card of the twenty-two is the Wheel of Fortune which as it turns either chains us to its endless cycle or throws us off into liminal space. Then in the midst of this liminal space sits Death representing the end of the old, the loss of knowing that creates the necessary condition for transformation. Interestingly, Death sits aside the Devil who then represents the new emerging, as old blocks are shattered after death. So in the tarot, supporting our earlier consideration, the Devil is very much involved in the cycle of death and life.

The tarot, representing as it does the journey of every man and every woman through life, consistently asks us to face the universal inevitability of death, the equality of all people facing death, and the meaningless of the trappings of life such as fame and wealth which are no guard against death's final touch.[30]

*

Sacred Space

Wherever you are, be it in your own home, in a crowded street, in a hospital – all of these places are sacred. Your home is sacred because it is not only your physical resting place and a shelter from the elements, but also because it is the container for your dreams and aspirations, and a place to lick your wounds and just be yourself; in fact, the more you think about it, the more reasons you can come up with for saying your home is sacred. But what of a crowded street, how can that be sacred? Think of all those people, all living their lives as best they know how, all 'out in the world' facing the opportunities and challenges, the ups and downs of social interaction, the highs and lows of success and failure at the different tasks they are undertaking; that sounds pretty sacred to me for it is the energy of life in action. A hospital is also sacred for many reasons, not least because it is a place of healing. So we can easily find reasons to assert the sacredness of any location but underlying all of this, wherever we are, is the sacredness of the earth, our planet beneath our feet without which we would not have life.

You cannot make a place sacred because everywhere is sacred already, but what you can do is to connect with its sacredness and draw it into yourself. Some people think everyone dies in the 'right place' for them, which may be true (and in a philosophical sense, surely is) but that does not absolve us from the responsibility of not necessarily choosing where we die but of making sacred the place where we do meet death. Of course, the place where each person dies is sacred but how much more so if at that very time you are connected yourself to the sacredness of this place.

The following practice is a way of opening up to a sense of the sacredness of your space.

Reflection

Simply say to yourself: this is my sacred space.

Be aware of and connect with the earth energies beneath you;

Be aware of and connect with the guardians or spirits of the place;

Be aware of your connection with these energies that will be with you at this time.

Imagine you are at the centre of a circle that is as large as your furthest perceptions.

Imagine a strong cord coming from the middle of your body down into the centre of earth.
Imagine there is a hook or anchor on the end of the cord, and feel it attach to the earth very firmly.

Imagine, sense and feel the presence of the guardians and angels of this place where you are and welcome their presence now.

Expand your awareness to the immediate environment and nearby countryside. Silently ask the good spirits of this countryside to be present for you throughout your life and at your death, to assist at this time.

Return to full awareness of your physical body. Tune into your heart, and be aware of the energy there. Breathe into your heart centre now, feeling energy building up. Let your heart centre open as much as is appropriate for you right now.

Allow yourself to dwell in this place for as long as you wish.

If it feels right, when you are ready bring your awareness back to your current physical situation and affirm the rightness of your presence in life. It is not yet your time to die.

Repeat this exercise as often as you wish. When it is your time to die, simply detach the anchor from the centre of the earth and let yourself go.

❊

PART 2

DEATH

*"For what is it to die but to stand naked in the wind
and to melt into the sun? And what is it to cease breathing,
but to free the breath from its restless tides, that it may rise
and expand and seek God unencumbered? Only when you
drink from the river of silence shall you indeed sing.
And when you have reached the mountaintop,
then you shall begin to climb. And when the earth
shall claim your limbs, then shall you truly dance."*

Kahlil Gibran [31]

The Dying Process

Our bodies are unstable. All the cells that make us up need a continuous input of energy without which they don't work anymore. This energy is supplied by the synthesis in cells of various products that come from oxygen and the breakdown of foodstuffs. If we stop the blood supply which carries this nutrition to various parts of the body, or we interfere with the removal of waste products leaving the cells, then the cells will be damaged and die. The loss of oxygen is particularly critical: most cells can maintain some level of life energy but they cannot store oxygen, they need a continuous supply of this, so even a momentary interruption of the oxygen supply can lead to their demise.

Different cells in different parts of the body can actually last longer depending upon their functions, so in skin tissues, for example, cells survive for several hours whereas some of the cells in the brain can survive only five minutes or so without oxygen. This is mostly due to the differences in their metabolic rate but perhaps it also points to a deeper meaning. Large numbers of cells in, for instance, a leg could die but it would not necessarily lead to the death of the person, but death of cells in the brain will at least damage the control centres of the brain, perhaps affecting intellectual capacity or the ability to control functions such as breathing. To animate your body you need a freshly fed, vibrant amount of brain cells. Who is this 'you' that does this, that animates your body through the agency of your brain centres?

✳

The Body Remains

After death our bodies cool down. How fast and to what degree depends upon external factors such as what environment we are in, what clothing we are wearing, and so on, and internal factors such as our body temperature at time of death, variations in our somatic cycles, the presence of disease, and so on. How hot life is, no wonder we cool down afterwards. Well, wouldn't you? You will! All that thinking, creating mental energy – we speak sometimes of igniting thoughts whilst our thoughts are igniting us. All that feeling, hot with anger, aflame with passion, on heat, being burnt up with envy – we know that those of us who appear to be or claim to be cool are as hot as the rest of us underneath. All that physical activity, burning calories, buzzing about with too much to do, getting hot under the collar and having night head sweats – to say nothing of a fiery spirit. The cool breeze, the calm breath, the gentle tease of an 'easy' death – how comforting to our over-hot selves, bustling with activity.

For us humans, like other mammals but unlike most other animals, along with the body temperature falling after death, rigor mortis also sets in, usually after around two hours or so, sometimes earlier. Blood is not being pumped around the body anymore and because of the subsequent changes in the oxygen and protein available to muscles, they gradually stiffen. Anytime from twelve hours, sometimes less if it is very warm, sometimes as much as a week later, these effects disappear due to the body's decomposition.

Rigor mortis means the rigidity of death which is the opposite of the flexibility of life, or is it? If we focus on just the corpse, the physical body no longer animated by spirit, of course this is medically correct, but does the flexibility of life come from the collection of bones, muscles and tissues that make up the body, or does it come from the animating spirit within, the consciousness that moves the body? Perhaps this consciousness is 'local', it resides entirely within the body and when the body dies it dies away with it. Perhaps it is 'non-local', the body being a vehicle for its manifestation so when the body dies, consciousness experiences the change but remains constant. You make your choice and live with it – and die with it, too.

Another change after death is that the body starts to change in colour, getting paler and paler. This happens because the substance in the blood that causes it to clot stops working after death so gravity pulls all the blood in the body downwards, forming a pool, sometimes within the body, sometimes leaking out of the body. The characteristic paling of a corpse can be seen fairly soon after death. By twelve hours or so later the corpse will be blotchy and patterned, quite how depending on its position, how much pressure is put on it, and of course the cause of death and the environment in which the person died.

Cosmeticians in the mortuary may colour the body to make it more palatable to look at, especially for the family and loved ones, but there is no disguising the absence of a motivating consciousness. It is our consciousness that brings colour not only to our physical bodies but also to our lives generally. When we feel cut off and depressed we feel – and are perceived by others as – colourless. We are pale in comparison to our former selves. You might think, then, that if you are not feeling depressed when you die you might keep your colour; you will, and you may take it with you – leave the pale stuff for the corpse which is no longer you. Whatever you have experienced throughout life, it has been colourful – not always comfortable colours, of course, the red anger and sad blues come to mind – but with colour rather than without. Now, without life, without colour, your body is free to rest, to relax pumping blood, let go of a million unconscious activities that kept it alive for your spirit to colour, and to be free to fade into … the colour of the earth.

The fall in temperature and commencement of rigor mortis happen before the decomposition of the body starts. Nothing is wasted, it is a moment's respite, a time for the soul to depart without encumberment, before the most metabolically active cells start to digest themselves, and be eaten by their own enzymes. As this continues to happen they lose their structure and start collapsing. Pretty much at the same time various bacteria commence digesting the remains and the body starts putrefying. We've had these bacteria in our bodies whilst still alive, those that live in the colon, for instance. They are not just sitting there waiting to eat us, we have been supplying them with digested food stuff which they have helped further digest, clean and prepare for evacuation. They have done us good service and now, when we are able to relax and leave, we can let them continue to work in our bodies, now to clear up the mess and prepare the corpse for recycling.

The bacteria that inhabit our bodies digest the corpse, breaking molecules down, degrading all the carbohydrates, proteins, acids and so on in the corpse to produce gases which add to the colour changes, odours and bloating, and general liquefaction of the corpse. Whilst this is going on, air bound bacteria and fungi arrive from outside and contribute to the decay process. If we could look closely enough we might see some of these bacteria and fungi at work whilst we are still alive (however thoroughly we scrub ourselves!). Already happening whilst we are still alive, the process accelerates once the body is dead. Bring it on, let my corpse be food for others as others have been food for me.

Putrefaction and decay particularly increase when the juices from their early stages have drained away as everything is then in a relatively dry state. As what remains of the corpse becomes drier and drier we are left with a skeleton – all the soft parts having decayed away. That isn't the end though, because the hard tissues (bone and teeth) are also decomposing (ask a dentist how this is already happening too.) It takes a lot longer but the bone and teeth are invaded by bacteria, algae and fungi that have the power to penetrate hard tissue, excreting enzymes or acids, slowly decomposing the mineral substance that was once a human body. The older the bones, the more cracked and disintegrated they become. Remember how it was in that aging body and rejoice that you don't have to experience the bones not merely slightly out of place but now cracking, collapsing, turning eventually to dust. Wipe that dust off the window ledge that came in the window earlier and remember your distant ancestors who once animated these particles.

✳

The Moment of Death

How do you know when somebody is actually dead? To define the exact moment of death has always been something of a problem. We might choose to say it is when the animating spirit has departed, but that's not the answer medical science looks for – because we are referring to the death of the body (alive) after which it turns into a corpse (dead.) So when does a body become a corpse? Some have said it is when the heart beat and breathing stop, but sometimes – certainly in modern conditions – a persons heart and breathing have stopped yet they are revived. As we do not (yet?) have the ability to bring people back to life, this must mean they were not actually dead, despite the 'right' signs. So any definition to do with heart beat and breathing is no longer adequate. With the abundance of various different life support devices, bodies can be kept alive even without a functioning heart or lungs. It is no wonder then that we have ethical debates about what constitutes a living being.

Let's remember there is no such thing as a non-living being – clearly 'to be' you have to be alive. So as we move on through this new century, we can expect there to be an ever growing number of people with artificial organ transplants, pacemakers, and various other pieces of equipment in their body which keep them alive. These people are not being kept artificially alive because they are alive; so what if we increase the implanted parts – when does a body become artificial? Is it when, for instance, more than fifty per cent of it is made up of non-living artefacts? If we carry this to a logical conclusion, even if the physical body is completely replaced by an artificial body, the presence of consciousness is still likely. If we were to invent a preferable artificial form in which our consciousness could exist, perhaps we would be better off. If that sounds outrageous, consider our ancestors' bodies (human and pre-human) compared to ours.

A more modern definition of death, termed biological or sometimes brain death, is when there is no longer any electrical activity in the brain and the body is in a persistent vegetative state. This definition depends upon being able to ascertain if it is a permanent end of consciousness and not just a transient one as occurs during sleep or more especially during coma. Some people argue that only the neocortex is necessary for consciousness and that only electrical activity in that part of the brain should be considered in deciding whether someone is dead or not. There again, some people think that death happens at a predestined moment decided by a deity and, quite frankly, the evidence for either view is limited. No one has ever returned from death to notify us of our mistake, only those we have thought dead when they were not have returned to life. Perhaps being dead is not a finality but more wisely viewed as a pathway that, although once you set off down it you are unlikely to return, it is two way and some people come back to the beginning of the path even when they've been a long, long way (if not the whole way.)

Imagine holding a mirror in front of someone's mouth to see if any condensation forms on the mirror. If yes, it shows that there is breathing so the person is alive; if not they are dead. We have clearly gone beyond that method now, but we may have reached a point in modern life where it is very difficult to ethically and scientifically decide exactly when death might really occur. We cannot return to such a flawed method of detection as the mirror, and we may as well accept that, for now anyway, the best definition of death is the cessation of electrical activity in the whole brain. However, instead of relying on scientific methodology, we can also be patient, wait and watch, allowing the spirit, if it is that time, to slip gently away, or if it is not that time, to dwell in its necessary underworld.

The pressure on beds in the health service, or even in a hospice, the distress of loved ones, the belief systems of others, all may contribute to a too speedy decision in the marking of this vital chapter in the person's life (whether they recover or not.) In 2005, the case of Teri Schiavo[32] was a media event as different groups argued whether her artificial life support should be turned off or not. If someone is on a life support system and it is turned off it is said that seven minutes is enough to stop any further activity of any kind in the cerebral cortex. Seven minutes in a timeless space, the borderlands (or bardos) between life and – whatever might come next.

We can call the end of all life processes in an organism 'somatic death' to distinguish it from 'physical death' where the body has died but the consciousness might be in some way be continuing. Even when somebody's heart and lungs have stopped working so they are physically (or clinically) dead, they might not be somatically dead.

Most of us have heard at some point the anecdotal references to people supposedly dead who have come back to life. Being buried alive is a particular concern for many people and was even more so when burial was more prevalent. There are, apparently, authentic tales of coffins being dug up and scratches being found on the wood on the inside of the lid of the coffin, suggesting some people came back to life after being buried. Of course, this means they were never really dead.

In Victorian days, some coffins were buried with little bells and flags on the surface that had a connecting string into the coffin so if the person in the coffin did wake up they would be able to signal the outside world they had not really died. In a 2007 issue of Time magazine, a case was reported of a man whose electrical activity had virtually ceased, having been in a coma for a long period, just before the final moment of death sitting up in bed and quite brightly saying goodbye to each of his relatives at the bedside.[33]

There are other unusual cases where an apparently dead person has come back to life: for instance, people who have been found unconscious under icy water have been kept cold until they could be properly resuscitated, and have miraculously survived. Some attempts are being made to cryogenically freeze corpses so that if in the future science finds ways of curing what killed them they can be brought back to life. If there is an animating spirit, will it have stayed there whilst the corpse awaited its revival, or will the spirit return at that moment – or might it not return at all?

Seeing as how our ideas about when death occurs have changed quite considerably, it is likely that we will be continuing to evaluate when someone is dead, particularly as we get more and more techniques for reviving people after longer periods of apparent death. After many years of being frozen, however, I wouldn't be at all surprised if the body of the person – whatever their essence may be, whether local or non-local in nature – will have given up the ghost!

We can tell when someone is approaching death, as there are fairly typical signs to indicate this. Speaking less, feeling sleepy and lethargic, being confused when awake, decreasing interest in, then not wanting food and liquid intake, having difficulty swallowing, periods of paused breathing which may alternate with rapid breathing, noisy breathing, sounding like there is something stuck in the throat, the extremities becoming colder, blotches appearing at the extremities, loss of bowel and bladder control, falling blood pressure – and moving towards a space where they will be alone – at last, at one with their own self, consciousness enfolding into itself, becoming detached from the physical and moving into the sea of all consciousness where each droplet entirely depends upon the whole and yet remains uniquely itself. Give thanks that after a life of suffering – and joy – there is peace before return.

✳

Different Cultures

A s you would expect, different cultures have different ideas about what to do with corpses, but in many cultures the body goes through some kind of ritualised disposal which usually involves one of the four 'elements of the wise', that is fire, water, air or earth.[34] The best known fire ritual is cremation, which might take place in a specially constructed chamber or in the open air, even with living relatives joining the corpse on the pyre. The earth ritual is burial or entombment which might involve a grave, a crypt, mound or barrow, mausoleum or even pyramid. In some cultures, in the past, efforts were made to retard the decay processes, such as with mummification and embalming. This is also a modern concern for some people, particularly in the (over-) developed world where bodies may be preserved in case of future revival possibilities.

Fire and earth are the two most commonly used elements for disposing of corpses, but sometimes there are air rituals, such as the sky burial of Tibet where corpses are left on high ground for the air (and birds of prey!) to dispose of. In fact in some cultures, such as the Tibetan[35], there is a belief that birds of prey are the carriers of souls, either to heaven or in-between incarnations. On a pragmatic level, perhaps air burial might occur where the ground is too hard to dig. As the body is only an empty shell after death, air burial may also be seen as an act of compassion and kindness, to leave the corpse for animals to consume.

There are also water rituals, in particular burial at sea which is usually found in fishing or naval communities. Some modern forms of funeral may involve more exotic combinations of elements. Some people have had space burials where rockets launch their cremated remains into orbit. When the rocket re-enters the atmosphere and burns up, at least in principle the ashes of the person in the rocket will be spread throughout the whole atmosphere. You can also arrange for someone's ashes to be made into a diamond and then put into jewellery. Someone might end up sparkling more after death than they did before! Many ancient cultures who used the element classification actually noted five rather than four elements, the fifth being spirit. Then the fire, water, air or earth ritual may not only be for disposal of the corpse but also a final elemental freeing of the fifth element.

So, to summarise, with a dead body we can:

- donate it to medical research;
- donate it for organs and so on for living people;
- have the body buried in a woodland (useful for compost, and involves no embalming chemicals, toxins released into air from burning, etc);
- it can be cremated;
- it can be made into a gem (the remains are cooked, carbonised and pressed into gems which are then made into rings, bracelets or other jewellery);
- the body may be shot into space (from where it returns to burn up in the atmosphere);
- a corpse may have a sea burial;
- a body can be freeze-dried then shattered and made into a mulch for growing trees;
- and many other ingenious ideas that we humans may invent.

A personified figure of death features in some way or another in most cultures and in various myths and legends. In Western imagery, death is often depicted as a skeleton carrying a scythe, as in the popular tarot card image of death we explored earlier. This depiction has even found its way into a modern computer game, The Sims, where if one of the characters dies the 'grim reaper' appears and offers the character an opportunity to purchase their life back. The player is able to imagine making deals with death, perhaps the ultimate avoidance of the existential truth of the presence of death throughout life. How many lives do you have left in the game you are playing? Truly only the one you are now living and dying.

*

Elements of Death

Thanatology, a term invented by a Russian biologist, is the science of the study of death.[36] The field of investigation of this science includes not only things to do with the biological changes that occur at death but also the social, psychological, emotional, legal and ethical factors involved. Underneath, when we face our inner truth, we are all thanatologists.

Some believe that if people are hopelessly ill they should be actively assisted by doctors to commit suicide so they can die painlessly and with dignity. It seems somewhat strange that countries have laws that are against this practice, whereas they will send to war young adults who haven't had a life yet. In some countries, Holland and Switzerland being prime examples, physician assisted suicides are technically legal and do happen. Curiously, these are also countries that tend to not participate in warlike activities. If people can freely and clearly request assistance to die, who are we to say they cannot, especially when we are not considering 'active euthanasia' (where people are fatally ill and put to death without their consent) but rather situations involving individuals who are choosing to die?

Various groups in history, and particularly in recent times, have been pressing for a legal right to die. On the basis that all the life sustaining treatments we have, although they might prolong life, they may also prolong suffering, perhaps it is wrong that people are kept alive when it would be somewhat better if they were allowed to die. Euthanasia, defined as the induction of death by gentle or passive means at the behest of the dying person, is illegal in most countries. You might think your body is yours to choose what to do with, or if you are incapacitated that you are in the safe hands of your relatives who will be able to make an informed and compassionate decision on such a matter. Not so, in fact various ethical and legal controversies mean even those people who would definitely benefit from euthanasia are not necessarily allowed to die. The increasing use of a Living Will attests to this concern and seems like a sensible procedure if you are at all concerned in this way.

Thanatologists have identified several stages in the process of death as usually experienced by dying people:
• Denial and isolation (no not me)
• Anger rage envy and resentment (why me)
• Bargaining (if I am good…)
• Depression (what's the use)
• Acceptance.

Most people find these stages do not necessarily occur in any particular order and often go along with all kinds of other feelings, either of hope on the one hand, anguish and terror on the other. But like the individual who is dying, friends and family often go through these or similar stages before reaching acceptance.

Bereavement may occur before the loved one dies and this may lessen or defuse later stress, but after the death has occurred, bereavement tends to be longer and more severe, especially if the death was unexpected. Mourners may cry (or resolutely hold back their tears), have difficulty sleeping (or in some cases staying awake), they may lose their appetite, feel alarmed, angry or aggrieved at being deserted, and they may become depressed and feel lonely. Whether the bereavement is short or long, eventually people generally regain their energy and start to restore ties to others.

Many people, even children, know that they are dying and being able to express their honest feelings can help them to accept this and, and being given safety and security, achieve a dignified and serene death. This can be assisted by therapists, hospital staff, clergy and so on helping the person talk about their feelings, thoughts and memories, and helping them deal with the anxiety with which friends and family are sometimes not able to cope and for which they should not have to take responsibility.

In most cultures, and well into the 20th Century in Europe and North America, most people died in their own homes, often following a brief illness. The family would almost certainly be present, or at least close-by, and after death there would be some kind of public ritual to mark the passing of the spirit of the newly deceased. But by the beginning of 21st century, in industrialised nations at least, death has become more private and seldom discussed. People now die later but also of more chronic diseases. In the United States, for instance, in the early 20th century most people died under fifty years of age, whereas now most die older than sixty-five. In very recent times in industrial nations there have been movements aimed at creating better condition for people to cope with death and dying, the hospice movement being paramount. Hospices were first established by religious orders in Europe in the middle ages to care for sick and dying pilgrims and have now become widespread throughout the world. There is also a movement towards providing resources for home care so that, along with pain control or prevention, people can have a more dignified death than is possible in a hospital. These are heartening, but it is still the case that the vast majority of dying people do not have access to such resources.

*

The Everlasting Self

Consider this: there are approximately six billion people on the planet today; about 50-100 million die each year, which is equivalent to about 1 million people dying each week, 200,000 each day, 1,000 each hour, or somewhere around 20 people die each minute.[37] Sit quietly with a clock in front of you and watch one minute pass, and reflect on the twenty or so people who die during this minute. Death is always with us, maybe death is waiting just behind your left shoulder, waiting to tap you, and when it does and you look round, you are facing your death.

Of course, this is a lot harder to understand or accept when someone dies prematurely, especially as an infant or child. Those who survive into old age do not necessarily become 'elders' in a developmental sense. Issues from earlier stages that have not been integrated may arrest the development of an individual acting out unintegrated physical, emotional and mental identifications. At least someone who lives to old age has had a chance with their life's tasks, unlike someone who dies younger. A major aspect of dealing with such deaths is to see our lives not only as individual but as part of a larger, collective unfolding of evolution. An individual spark of consciousness may be extinguished but the light of the Self is everlasting.

✳

Rites and Rituals

It is interesting to look into the dictionary definitions and etymology of the word death and it is fascinating that, printed onto A4 paper, the entry for death in the Oxford English Dictionary covers more than thirty pages, offering nineteen different meanings for the word death and a plethora of associated ways the word is used in combination with other words. The first definition given is that death is the act or fact of dying which may seem overly self-evident but if we reflect on it for a while it asserts a basic and inalienable fact – that death exists and it happens. That in itself is an existential truth underpinning all our investigation and/or denial of the 'act or fact of dying.'

Whatever people believe or don't believe about death, and whether there is an afterlife or not, after-death rites perform an important symbolic and sociological function for the survivor. Funeral rites and customs are performed more for the well being of the survivors than for the body of the dead person for whom such customs have clearly become irrelevant. Whether we are considering the physical level of such rites – the disposal of the body being paramount – or more abstract concerns – the persistence of the spirit or memory of the deceased especially – the importance of such activities cannot be over-emphasised.

In most societies, the body is prepared in some way before it is laid to rest. Archaeological evidence tells us, for instance, that some of our earlier ancestors stained dead bodies with red ochre, and most burial sites show signs of dressing the body with special garments or adorning it with ornaments and amulets. The Egyptians believed that by keeping the body intact there was a greater chance for the soul to pass into the next life and thus they developed their complex and effective procedures of mummification. It has a somewhat different aim than the embalming that happens in modern society which is so that the mourners do not have the confront the processes of putrefaction in the body of the deceased.

A funeral provides an occasion for ritual appropriate to the beliefs of the survivors and mourners and the society of which they are part. In some sects of Hinduism the widow might throw herself onto the burning pyre of her husband; in some ancient societies, slaves were buried with their owners, but generally the rituals and mourning rites associated with the actual disposal of the body are intended to be kind and uplifting for the mourners. This may even include a celebration not only of the life and passing from life of the dead, but also of the continuing life of the mourners. The death of a person considered special in a particular culture may be marked, for example, through the firing of weapons in a military salute. The remembrance of some people may be manifest through building monuments and special tombs but generally funeral customs of whatever kind are a symbolic representation of the values that prevail in a particular society more than the values attributed to a specific individual.

Even the emotions exhibited at a funeral relate to the customs of the society: in some places the mourners are expected to grieve very visibly and in some traditions mourners are specifically hired to weep and wail loudly at a funeral. On the other hand, in some societies complete silence might be the norm at the funeral rite. As with the rituals chosen for the funereal rites, the degree of emotions shown at a funeral is generally appropriate to the rules and morals of that society.

In spite of the wide variation in rites and rituals some anthropologists have noticed that four major elements are usually involved:
• colour symbolism;
• the treatment of hair;
• the inclusion of noise and drumming;
• preservation or cosmetic processes applied to the dead body.

In the West, we associate black with death whilst the Chinese associate white with death; hair is sometimes shaved off as a sign of grief, or allowed to grow as a sign of sorrow; by making a noise or drumming at funerals we excite the spirit world and chase off any negative energies; by processing the body in some way, even if only dressing it in Sunday-best clothing, we are showing the world that death has a symbolic as well as a literal significance, it's not necessarily the ending of life, even if it is the ending of the little life in this world.

Modern funeral practices in the West are sometimes seen as rather unnatural where, for instance, bodies are embalmed and cosmetically made up so they appear as natural and life-like as possible, so they don't upset the mourners or make them nauseous from the decaying corpse. Our modern Western funeral practices may even be seen as examples of capitalist exploitation (particularly in the case of some American funeral parlours.) The (American based) Encarta dictionary states: "[These practices]… are a sombre rite of passage that reflects American social and religious values concerning the nature of the individual and the meaning of life."

In the UK, the capitalist hold on the funeral market is evident when we consider this market is estimated to be worth more than a billion pounds annually. With something not much short of a million funerals taking place each year that's a thousand pounds or so per funeral. There are four thousand or so funeral directors in Britain, a profession that is surprisingly unregulated. Sometimes what appear to be well known and local family firms are actually part of larger organisations kept under the local name to give the illusion of a traditional and local service as many families remain loyal to the same undertakers over the years. This is, to say the least, a rather shrewd marketing practice. Regarding tradition, as the Victorians invented the coffin, the hearse, the black clothes, the granite memorial, the burial grounds, the drapes and most of the jobs of the funeral director, and as we've been brought up to regard funerals as if that is the way they have to be, it is not too surprising that many of us fall for the marketing techniques. People arranging funerals are often very vulnerable and in need of a measure of protection. Even if they are not happy with the service they get from a funeral director, they might be too upset to complain, and rather put the whole affair behind them, so caution is truly required in this area.

This is not to say funeral directors are all callous, money-hungry capitalists. Whilst the financial aspects of their service cannot be denied, the vast majority of such companies are staffed by caring and considerate people whose aim is to support, comfort and make as easy as possible this difficult transition for the survivors of the dead person. At the very least, it could be argued that by taking care of the arrangements for the disposal of the corpse and so on, they are making the space and time necessary for the survivors to mourn more thoroughly and effectively, without having to be burdened by the logistics of the situation.

✳

Comforting Others

What should you say when someone has died? One of the most difficult things to do after someone close to you dies is to contact other people close to them – relatives, friends, and so on, to tell them the news. You know you will make them unhappy and who wants to do that to someone, and yet you have no choice but to tell them. In these circumstances the truth is most people don't know what to say, so apart from the shock and condolences, etc, there isn't much to say. More important is the feeling conveyed and creating a field of positive support.

First and foremost, if you can, is to offer help (and if you are the one offered the help, to accept it). Maybe someone else can phone or write to people on your behalf to let them know the news. Good friends always ask first 'what can I do?', not 'is there anything I can do?' which is one step removed.

It is important though to convey something and this is probably best done through a card or letter. It doesn't matter to say anything particular, or the 'right thing', just to let the grieving person know you are thinking of them, are with them. Part of this is not to try to explain anything, or to tell the bereaved you know how they feel – you might, but they don't need to hear that, they don't need speculation about how you feel. The bereaved do not have the energy to cope with other people's feelings so give them a break and keep your feelings and ideas of how they must be feeling to yourself.

Finally, behave normally, calmly, offering reassurance by showing that the world goes on. Don't pretend nothing has happened, that would be denial, but include what has happened, remind the person that you, their life and the world goes on not despite but because of and including the bereavement.

✳

Boundaries of Death

Death is sometimes described as being a 'boundary situation' – that is, it inevitably involving a change from one state to another. This is obvious, of course, but we can use it to our advantage. It has been said, for instance, that cancer is the greatest cure for 'psychoneurosis' and it is true that our worries about everything from getting bad luck through walking under a ladder to inner feelings of physical inadequacy are put back into their rightful place once we are confronted by death. Existence cannot be postponed, and the same is true for death which is an integral part of existence. If the imminent presence of death helps us to count our blessings then it serves us; why wait until death is literally, physically imminent for it is right here with you now. Now is the time to count your blessings. Do it now.

Reflection

List on eight separate cards your immediate answers to the question: who am I?

After writing these cards, review your answers and arrange the cards in order of importance, putting answers that feel closest to your core at the bottom, more peripheral ones on top.

Study the top card and reflect on what it would be like to let go of this attribute... consider it for a while then place the card face down and go on to the next card.

Continue with this until you have divested yourself of all eight attributes or answers to the question: Who am I?

When all the cards have been processed in this way, simply and quietly reflect on what you are experiencing... stay with this for some time, then, when you are ready, turn the cards one by one back over and consider whether you want to take on each definition of yourself or not. Choose wisely!

✳

Metaphorical Death

There are two types of death: literal and metaphorical. A literal death is when the body stops functioning and consciousness ceases; a metaphorical death refers to times of transition and change, when you are at the end of one cycle in your life and at the beginning of another. Of course, literal death, as well as being the end of this life may also be the beginning of some other type of existence, but we don't know for sure. Without denying hope, or any possibility that there is something to experience after death, whilst we are still alive it can seem better to assume that death is the end which it certainly is of life as we know it. That way death, rather than defocusing us through fear, can help focus us in the here and now.

Being alive is being incarnate, in the flesh. Dying is about learning to give up what you have embodied. Death is giving up form: that is, giving up being embodied and disembodied, being bounded and unbounded. No more duality – once you're dead there is no more life or death!

Death is about the emergence of the unknown, about facing the unknown. For your ego, death is about the threat of not being. In death, as both being and not being are absent, there is actually nothing for your ego to fear.

Stanley Keleman[38], the psychologist, defines five ways in which people may not fully surrender to the death experience. A morbid death involves fear and/or pain and death is seen as an executioner, something to avoid and deny. A fool's death is about not accepting death, thinking we shall come back, that death is just a rebirth. A martyr's death is one of noble sacrifice, important in some way beyond the immediate life of the individual themselves. A hero's death is where death is experienced as an enemy to fight. The hero aims to die nobly and bravely. A wise person's death is one of resignation. As it is inevitable, the wise person reckons it is best to accept it and view it as a sleep, a blessing, a return to nature, and an end of the tasks of life.

In whatever way you view it, however, so long as you are still here (that is, alive) your life has not ended. The corollary is then, of course that when you are dead, your life has ended. Because death is inevitable, it has to involve some kind of surrender. This surrender to death, however, has to be really experienced and not overlaid with the bizarre, senseless, victim-like, flamboyant, or submissive ways that Keleman delineates with his classification of approaches to death in a morbid, foolish, martyred, heroic, or even wise person's defensive ways.

Reflection

Consider for a moment: how good are you at surrendering?

How are you at not surrendering *for* something or surrendering *to* something but just surrendering?

You might then like to try the following visualization that involves imagining yourself surrendering to the ocean:

Relax and imagine you are on a beach, a long, empty, warm, beautiful beach ... really take time to picture yourself there, and notice what you feel and what you sense...
what can you see? hear? smell? taste? how do you feel?...

Walk slowly into the ocean, deeper and deeper until you have to start swimming ... let yourself go, even if you cannot usually swim well, today trust that you can swim safely and strongly out into the deep water...

Really experience the sensation of swimming out to sea, for no purpose other than for the enjoyment of it ... the experience of being in the ocean is all there is, all you need at this moment...

Now simply relax and float in the warm, blue salt water which holds you buoyant and safe...

Let yourself surrender in any way you desire to the embrace of the sea ...

You don't need to do anything to surrender to the ocean in this way, simply be yourself ...

Stay with that experience for as long as you wish, but when you are ready do the following procedure to bring yourself back to full awareness of where you are and your current situation.

Slowly bring your consciousness back where you are, here today ... feel the weight of your body supported by what is under you, feel your presence in the room here, right now ... open your eyes ...

※

Design for Dying

Stephen Levine[39], in his book "Who Dies?", quotes a rather beautiful description of the process of death which uses the four elements we met earlier:

"The hardness of the body begins to melt... The boundaries of the body, its edge, are less solid. There is not so much a feeling of being 'in' the body. One is less sensitive to impression and feelings ... As the earth element continues to dissolve into the water element there is a feeling of flowingness, a liquidity ... a feeling of fluidity.

"As the water element begins to dissolve into the fire element, the feelings of fluidity become more like a warm mist. The bodily fluids begin to slow, the mouth and eyes become dry, circulation slows ... a feeling of lightness ensues.

"As the fire element dissolves into the air element, feelings of warmth and cold dissipate, physical comfort and discomfort no longer have meaning... A feeling of lightness, as of heat rising, becomes predominant. A feeling of dissolving into yet subtler and subtler boundarylessness.

"As the air element dissolves into consciousness itself there is a feeling of edgelessness. ... there is no longer the experience of bodily form or function but just a sense of vast expanding airiness, a dissolving into pure being."

Timothy Leary[40] in his book "Design For Dying" offers a different but equally inspiring description:

"Any pain that one will suffer comes first. One will instinctively, automatically, biologically struggle to remain corporate. But your body goes limp, your heart stops, and no more air flows in or out. Sight and tactile feelings go. Your hearing is the last thing to go ... The final moment is not painful. Your identity drifts away but you still exist. Your brain is about to have the most amazing trip ever...

" ... when the body stops functioning, consciousness advances to the nervous system, where it belonged all our lifetime. Consciousness just goes home to the genetic code where it belongs. The genetic code brought us to the planet and she will help us escape from this planet across interstellar infinity to join our family. When consciousness leaves the body, neurological existence within a twenty-billion-cell ecstatic system becomes what we call infinite. When consciousness leaves the nervous system and fuses with the genetic code we receive all life since and before our embodiment."

✳

Heart Centre

The following meditation is designed for both the dying and their family and friends and cannot be over-used. Apart from its centring and relaxing aspects, it is a very powerful technique to enable you to tune into your energy. Do not be alarmed if you don't know what 'heart energy' means, or even if you don't believe in 'such things' – the exercise will work anyway, on whatever level you take it.

Reflection

Make yourselves as comfortable as you can and let your attention turn inwards. You do not have to breathe in any special way, but watch your breath as it comes into your body, turns, then passes right out again. As you breathe out, you might like to let go of any tensions in your body of which you are aware.

Imagine you are standing in a beautiful garden, facing the setting sun which is gently warming your face.

You can hear birds singing. In the distance you can hear the faint voices of children, happily playing.

You feel your body relax.

As the sun warms your face, it also warms your chest.
As it does so, you become aware of your heart. A bird chirps nearby, sharing in your stillness...

You take a deep breath – do it – and feel your heart open to the warmth of the sun.

There is a tingling of pleasure in your legs as you feel yourself firmly rooting into the warm, nourishing earth.

You turn your face up to the sun and you enter a deeper silence, a stillness in which your heart is bathed with light.

Breathe the healing light into your heart. Do this for as long as you like, then, when you are ready open your eyes.

✳

PART 3

AFTERLIFE

*"The body is not me; I am not caught in this body,
I am life without boundaries, I have never been born
and I have never died ... Birth and death are only a door
through which we go in and out. Birth and death
are only a game of hide-and-seek. So smile at me and take
my hand and wave good-bye. Tomorrow we shall meet
again or even before. We shall always be meeting
again at the true source, always meeting again
on the myriad paths of life.."*

Thich Nhat Hanh [41]

Afterlife and Incarnation

A very large number of people on the planet believe in some sort of afterlife and just because it cannot be scientifically proven doesn't stop them believing. We mostly agree that there's something rather than nothing after we die. But what it is – we certainly don't all agree on that, nor ever have done. An afterlife infers a continuation of existence, usually in some spiritual form that can be experienced. After all, if you're not experiencing anything it wouldn't be much of an afterlife at all.

Innumerable people, religions and cultures have put forward evidence for there being life after death, some of it compelling but none of it conclusive. You may believe in an afterlife and find evidence to support your belief, but that doesn't prove it is true. That is the nature of belief – and the afterlife. Can you trust what someone else tells you about what happens in the afterlife? Many billions of people do, or at least, on the surface, apparently do. Actually, of course, many adherents to a religion do not necessarily hold the beliefs that are part of their religion. There are Catholics, for example, who believe in reincarnation and contraception despite it being contrary to their church's beliefs; there are Buddhists who amass abundant possessions and are not charitable; and not every Muslim believes the teachings of the Koran on the life after death experience.

What do people believe? One very popular notion, often attributed to the testimony of people who have had near-death experiences, is that we enter a tunnel, move towards a bright light and have close ancestral relatives at hand. Perhaps it is a very meaningful and deep experience of DNA consciousness, but for some it is proof of an afterlife. Indeed, as some people have this vision not in near-death experiences but during out-of-body experiences when unconscious, it is common enough an experience to believe it happens – but how we interpret the experience might depend upon our preconceived notions of an afterlife. I started to write 'the afterlife' there rather than 'an afterlife' showing me how deeply ingrained such introjected belief systems can be: that 'afterlife' requires a definite rather than an indefinite article to precede it.

Some individuals have revelatory experiences that prove to them there is life after death. Maybe they meet a loved one who has died, or are guided by a remote entity that appears to be a dead person. Some people remember past lives and a few even recall future ones – sounds strange, but is remembering a future life really that much different from remembering a past one? We have to live with the paradox that as time does not really exist, certainly not in the way we experience it, that we may not exist now, never mind in the future or past. But if we assume we do exist (and we can always apply the 'pinch me' technique to check this out) then our 'exit' is bound to be both important to us – and, whether acknowledged or not, a fearful possibility – no probability – no, certainty!

Some people remember past incarnations, and some people – much fewer, but they do exist – are able to substantiate their claims. I saw the film of a young boy in India who was certain he had lived before in a certain town with his wife, and had been killed in an automobile accident outside his shop. Frustrated with his insistence, his parents took him to the said town; they found the shop, the wife – who was incredibly sceptical until the young boy whispered something in her ear that only she could know – and she could confirm her husband had been killed in an accident outside the shop. We might surmise the dying man's consciousness somehow was transferred into the boy when he was a baby; that somehow his memory was imprinted in some kind of collective consciousness which the boy happened to tune into – and it starts to sound more incredible than just accepting what the majority of us humans have accepted in one form or another for all these years – that this one life isn't everything and there could just as easily be a life before this one as one to follow.

What of the Tibetan monks who search for a boy who will recognise the religious possessions of a recently dead lama?

They search high and low until they find a baby boy who chooses the 'right' objects from a mixed pile. That he recognises his instruments from a previous life proves he is the reincarnation of the dead lama. Perhaps if they checked out the objects with other boys one of them would be bound, by chance, to eventually choose out the right objects, but does that mean that the first boy is not really the reincarnated lama? Not at all, because reincarnation might not operate in the linear and esoterically connected way we believe. As we don't know for certain that there is or is not a life after death, then we also must admit that we do not know how a reincarnating lama, should such a thing exist, might select his next incarnation.

There are those who don't believe in any kind of life after death, and it may be useful to consider if it is possible for there not to be an afterlife. At the very least, whether your body is buried on land or at sea, cremated (or even eaten by crows), components of your body will continue (even if we have to go to the atomic level of component to all agree on this.) The atoms that make up your body will surely make up something (or someone?) else again at some time or another (even if it is an almost infinitesimal time in the future.) But what of you – are you your body? Can you exist without a body (and do you exist within one)?[42]

✳

Immortal Soul

My soul is immortal so even if I pass away from this life this 'something greater than me' that I call 'soul' will continue. Well, it is comforting to believe that it isn't just a complete end when we die. Deeper though, we can realise nothing ends or begins, it transforms: and, really, if you are truly immortal would you want to be always you? Who's to say that as an immortal soul it isn't better to keep dying from one personality and body so you can move onto another; indeed, it would seem, from that viewpoint, to make complete sense. It is natural to desire immortality – the point is in taking care which parts of us we want to be immortal. If you reflect on this for a while, I imagine you probably won't include your personal identity as it is known to you now – but if you do, then I feel safe to assert it is your ego speaking. As children we develop egos so that we can have, in this life and in this body, a sense of personal and separate identity. We confer on ego the task of holding us together and, by implication, therefore, of keeping us alive. Anything that suggests otherwise and ego will step in and find some way of sabotaging or denying that we will cease to exist. Even as I write this, ego tried to make me write 'maybe' rather than will cease to exist. Maybe he's right, though I doubt it; what I do know is that I am less certain of the truth than he.

There are more ideas about what happens at the moment of death, not physically but spiritually and metaphysically, some of them presented as inalienable facts, than there are traditions and religion (because of course the adherents in many traditions and religions hold differing views from the established 'truth'.) As we have seen, belief that there is something after life entails believing there is at least some part of the person that survives the death of the body, even if this 'part' is re-assimilated into a universal or cosmic spirit. After all, it is impossible to be assimilated unless you were separate in the first place. Yet the deeper we look the more we discover we cannot even be sure that we are separate or whether this apparent life of individuality is an illusion. Many traditions, particularly from the East, either strongly hint at or even downright assert this to be the case – that what we call life is a dream. The implication is then that when we die (or follow some kind of other 'awakening' process) we will enter some 'after-life state' – that is, that there is something after death. Often coupled with such traditions is the notion that how we behave in life will affect not only the quality of our death but what happens to us in this 'after-life' and, if we are to re-incarnate, conditions ('lessons') we will have to deal with so that our 'awakening process' can continue. In some versions of Buddhism this life is seen as so painful that the ultimate 'reward' is to not be re-born as an individual ever again. Of course this is not through annihilation but through a hopefully blissful merging into the ultimate cosmic unity (the oneness from whence we arose, the state to which all our efforts are geared to help us to return.)

Think about this: that even the concept of 'self' is fundamentally flawed; really think about it hard for a while then ask yourself: from where does all this awareness arise?

✳

Cause and Effect

If how you live your life will affect (in some karmic or 'reward and punishment' system) what becomes of you after death (or when you are re-born), then it logically follows that, unless this is your first life ever, what you encounter and experience in this life must involve in some way 'karma' (or 'rewards and punishments') from your previous life or lives. I know people who having experienced terrible abuse in this life, usually in childhood, 'remember' terrible deeds they performed in a previous life which 'explains' why they have to suffer in this life. Surely if we reflect on this more deeply, we discover something else, more akin to a 'universal truth' than a simplistic reward and punishment notion.

Everything we do does have an effect, even if it is imperceptible to our usual senses. If I stand before a rock, shielding it from the sun for a whole day, it will feel cooler than if I had not shielded it. I have made the rock cooler. How much more easily we affect and are affected by other living creatures and, especially of course, by other fellow humans. We live in a sea of cause and effect and what goes out comes round (eventually, even if it takes aeons to do so.) In this way, karma can be seen as a field of inter-relatedness in which we all co-exist (that's us, other animals, plants and even rocks) in which nothing is ever forgotten or lost. Nothing is used up and gone and everything affects everything else. Take care, you are the most powerful being in your universe.

It is surprisingly unChristian to do good works to attempt to ensure 'going to heaven' rather than hell (or to accrue 'good karma' rather than bad.) St Paul asserted that we are only 'saved' through the grace of the deity and through faith in this, and not through any of our works.[43] Not all Christians agree with this, true, but it is a thoroughly embracing idea to consider that there is nothing you can do to deserve 'salvation' or heaven (and totally implicit in this there is nothing you can do to deserve eternal hell.) Living a good life doesn't ensure anything – anymore than not crossing the road will ensure you are not run down. Mother Theresa[44], for instance is made a saint by us humans (or specifically by one of us called the Pope) and we can do nothing but assume that if there is an afterlife she will be received positively. Yet the Pope is presumably making her a saint not because of her works but because of her faith; and the deity will only offer her salvation through his grace, not because of anything she has done or we have thought about her. Perhaps our little lives are not so important; and perhaps such reflections can help us realise this for, paradoxically, as we lose our self importance we come closer to a state in which, if we are lucky enough to have grace bestowed upon us, we can receive and use it fully. We might comfortably realise then that life is unimportant in determining our afterlife situation, but in each moment supremely important in determining our preparedness to face and receive whatever life and death bring us.

Universalists[45] say that we will all eventually be rewarded whatever we have or have not believed or done in our lives. Jehovah's Witnesses[46] suggest that there is no afterlife until at some future date those souls who have lived a good life will be resurrected (and those that are not will not suffer any kind of damnation but will be dead and gone forever.) The modern catechism of the Catholic church says that hell is not a punishment imposed on a sinner but is the state self-imposed by a non-believer through their lack of faith or belief in the deity. The corollary to that is of course that to believe, to truly believe, brings the experience of heaven alive in the believer now (and not just as a promise in the afterlife.) Some new-agers warn us to beware what we believe because it will come true (based on the ancient theory that energy follows thought.) Looks like what we believe makes all the difference so, reflect now for a while: what do you believe? If you are not happy with what you believe, how about considering how you might change this – it could make all the difference now, never mind in any possible afterlife.

✳

Possibilities

Go on, be good, what have you to lose? You never know, you might be judged at the gates of heaven and, because you were 'good', be allowed to enter; or what if reincarnation really happens? If you've been 'good' then you are likely to acquire a better new incarnation, be upgraded as it were. But then, you may ask, what's the point of all these successive incarnations? That at some distant point in the future you will be liberated – which means you won't have to keep on incarnating any more. This doesn't seem to offer a good press for living, does it? Maybe that's because what this theory really addresses is not life after death but life in life. Even if there was no after-life of any kind whatsoever, that when you died you are dead and gone, there would still be value in living a kind and altruistic life. For a start you might feel better about yourself than if you go round being unpleasant or unkind. So why can't we all be like this – caring for others and for ourselves in a selfless way, always acting with the good of the whole in mind?

Perhaps the Buddha was right in accusing desire for being the problem in our lives for it is dualistic, it separates the desirer from the desired and creates the conditions for greed, envy, jealousy, hate, and a host of other negative and very unliberating emotions. So long as we are separate we desire and so long as we desire we are attached and so long as we are attached we cannot be free. 'Help!' isn't really the best response, either, because there is no one around to help you – we're all in the same boat (or more exactly, on the same planet.) Yet, interestingly, this gives us the best clue yet to what we can do to get off the chain of successive and painful incarnations – to accept we are all in the same boat and to find a way to work together, to at least alleviate suffering and perhaps, through a joint effort, find a way to liberation.

This all assumes we are not yet free. Other traditions assert that we are already free – trouble is we have either forgotten this or somehow forget to notice it is already here. If I am already eternal at this moment, complete even in my inconsistencies and including all my hang-ups and neuroses, all of this is my eternal self, then there is nothing to fear in death anymore than there is anything to fear in anything else. Death then is no more than another change of scene. Considering how fleeting pleasure is in this world and, apparently anyway, how eternal death is, then maybe life can be experienced as a blissful repose before whatever comes next (not that it would matter if nothing did.) Further, if this is true for me it is equally true for everyone else – so in this life I can be kind and altruistic because I recognise my fellow travellers on this mysterious journey and to help any other individual is equally to help myself.

Is there ever any reason not to be kind and altruistic in your relations with others? Perhaps that is, at this moment, a question too far – perhaps we could use an affirmative statement here: there is never a reason to be other than kind and altruistic. And if we are recycled, our energy on whatever level you take it, from atoms and cells through parts of individual bodies, through souls to even spirit itself, then let's make this recycling process as effective as possible; after all, where (and as whom?) do you want to reincarnate? Better than you are now – or perhaps not better but able to fully realise just how good you've been all along.

Of course, as modern people clued up to the latest discoveries, theories and beliefs of our modern science, we can simply understand all our behaviour as a physical brain-based phenomena and there is no soul or spirit or anything else that will continue to exist separately from the physical body. The best science works in current hypotheses, accepting by them being 'current' that they have not always been held and will likely change as our knowledge and understanding of the world changes; and always stressing that a hypothesis is not a truth, it is a working idea, hopefully based upon the most up to date information. A current and widely known hypothesis is the notion that the human observer in a quantum experiment changes the result of the experiment merely by his observing presence.[47] Simply, the experimenter affects the experiment. Not such a strange notion really, one that most of us will readily accept, but the point for science is that this has been proven through experimentation so can take its place as a currently likely hypothesis.

If an experimenter affects the outcome then all experiments in science, including those concerning the existence or not of a soul or spirit separate from an individual living brain have been influenced by the consciousness, the mere presence of the researchers involved. Some mainstream scientists will not countenance the possibility of experiments that aim to prove (or disprove) an afterlife because their beliefs override their ability to fully hold such a hypothesis. Similarly some religionists will not accept the possibility of there not being an after-life. Is there really much difference between the two? Whether there is an afterlife or not, doesn't it make our life more interesting and even fruitful to reflect on and consider the possibility that we are wrong? It might even be that through questioning what is wrong with our beliefs and ideas we find out what is right about them. In other words, whatever you believe, you might be right after all.

So if you reflect on the possibility of an afterlife and weigh up all the evidence you could come to the conclusion, as some philosophers have, that as all claims about it are unverifiable it is meaningless to even think about it. Of course, all claims about there being or not being an afterlife are verifiable – if you die to find out. No one, of course, has proven they have been dead and returned to tell us what it is (or isn't) like. Again, however, we might consider ourselves to be eternal beings currently 'housing ourselves', as it were, in these bodies and this life; and as we exist eternally then to speculate on an after life is meaningless. It is equally meaningless to speculate on whether we might exist before or after life when we always exist whatever we are experiencing.

On the other hand, as everything I can think about an after life depends upon the activity of a physical brain, then it is impossible to prove anything exists outside the confines of that brain's activity. So what are we to believe? Maybe to accept we don't know, that we are inquisitive creatures who will always be trying to find out the truth (about not only the after life but pretty much everything else too) and that our best bet is to choose a belief that makes most sense to us, and remember that we have chosen it so we continue to have that belief rather than it taking us over and 'having us'.

✷

Approaching Darkness

When approaching darkness we may emulate, at least in part, those animals that hibernate through a winter period when nature turns inwards and the trees are asleep. If we can find the time to sit in the dark and quiet, in silence and reflection, then we can clear ourselves of all the passing emotions and troubles. Through entering the darkness we may find the way through that enables us to celebrate the re-emergence of light. In the darkness, we may even experience that complete and utter silence that transcends all ideas and experiences of life and death.

Reflection

What would you like to happen to your body after you die? What epitaph would you like written on your grave or memorial stone ?

What does your choice of memorial say about you?

Reflecting on these questions, what can you change in your life now that would make it more likely that you will be remembered the way you wish?

✳

Near Death Experience

Sometimes when people are clinically dead and then revived they report not only psychological and physiological experiences but also spiritual and transcendent ones. Whatever we believe about what actually is involved, most common is an 'out of body experience' (often shortened to OOBE), where people describe experiencing a sense of transcending the ego and personality, and sensing other beings (such as loved ones) coming to support and guide them. All this has a transcendent quality, is otherworldly in its nature. Such experiences are relatively common and more so since modern medicine has improved resuscitation techniques.

There are various versions of a tale in which a young man dies, experiences being out of his body and able to walk around amongst his relatives and friends, unseen by them but from his perspective able to fully see and hear all their interactions. The longer he is in this state the more he becomes distressed, feeling totally alone and worrying that he will be condemned to watch all these people interacting over aeons and aeons without himself ever being able to interact with them. His frustration is relieved when a hoofed, goat-like figure[48] comes to tell him he is not to die but will be returned to his body. Subsequently, he wakes and believes it has been a dream – until he looks out of the hospital window and sees the cloven footprints of the goat in the soft earth beneath the window and this awakens him to the possibility that there is more to dying (and being dead) than he had ever previously imagined possible.

Whilst the specifics of the experiences may be quite distinct, many people have near-death experiences which follow a progression from, initially, an awareness that one has 'died', through being out of the body, through various other possible scenarios, until, after a life review being given a 'reprieve' and retuned to the body, sometimes by now accompanied with a reluctance to return to the pain and difficulties that life entails.

If the experience lasts longer (or goes further towards death?) a 'tunnel' becomes more common, and in which people often encounter deceased loved ones or even older ancestors, disembodied spiritual figures who come to welcome and comfort the soul. At the furthest reaches of the tunnel, before entering the light, a special figure, a holy guardian angel or representative of the divine, reviews the individual's life and either returns them to this existence or aids them in passing through the 'doorway of light' at the end of the tunnel. No one (usually anyway) comes back from beyond this point, maybe suggesting that entering the light involves a cessation of individual consciousness as one merges into a collective spiritual well-being.

Comforting, isn't it, to imagine such things – and maybe that is all it is, the imaginings of the brain before its cessation, intended to comfort the person at their end. But what if these experiences are more than that and – even if not 'literal' as such, are at the very least representational of the experience we all may have at our individual death? That would be more than comforting because then the experience doesn't just inform the last moments of a dying person but can give us a deeper sense of connection and purpose even before we have an inkling of the approaching presence of death.

Maybe the thousands of scientists who claim as unreal all theories about consciousness that is independent of and can exist out of the body are right – but if they are, however deep their philosophical or analytical questioning, they cannot prove it to be so. Maybe the thousands of mystics throughout the ages are right that we are independent of our bodies and brains which we inhabit for the time we are in this life – but if they are, they cannot prove it to be so, either. As neither side can be proved to be correct in such a debate, it leaves us with a choice – and not just any choice, but the primary (and primal?) choice as to whether we believe we are just a body and only exist so long as this body is alive, or that we are more than that. Which choice serves you best?

From a scientific viewpoint this is not quite so straightforward. The scientific method, in all experiments and hypotheses, holds that we have to prove what cannot be seen rather than disprove what can. To all intents and purposes there is no proof for a continuation of existence beyond death and scientific method says so long as there is no irrefutable evidence then the onus is on those who believe there to be life after death to prove it. Considering this position, it is surprising – or maybe not so surprising! – that so many scientists will take a closed position on the subject and are not willing to even contemplate such a possibility; and also that many scientists experiment to 'prove' their 'scientific position' which, according to scientific methodology, they are under no obligation to prove one way or other as there is no evidence for one side of the discussion.

But is there no evidence? Many people will see a near death experience as akin to, or in actuality, an afterlife experience. For people holding this position, near death experiences cannot be explained by psychological or physiological causes and consciousness can and does function independently of brain activity. If we leave the theorists and scientists to their debates, however, we can perhaps move towards those people who have the most relevant information to give us – those who have actually undergone near death experiences. The vast majority of such individuals tend to be convinced that as their experience has been so real it tends to proves the existence of not only consciousness separate from the brain but of an afterlife. Even if this is 'scientifically unjustifiable' because it is only based on personal experience, more importantly it allows a sense of mystery to be alive within us and enables us to live positively with uncertainty.

People who have had near death experiences often experience long lasting spiritual effects; it is not that they suddenly decide that 'religion' was right after all, but their lives may be imbued with a new level of compassion, equanimity and connectedness. Even a strong reasoning faculty (which had previously been so certain of its position) can be opened to a wider and more open sense of investigation and reflection. If perhaps an experience has validity beyond the imaginings of a near dead brain, then just perhaps it may be reached again whilst still alive, a reflection that can lead to an ardent programme of spiritual contemplation which, although it may not confer eternal life, brings an inviolable peace that suffices to allow the individual to meet death the next time (from which they may not return) with a peaceful and soulful presence.

When it comes to our own experience, or that of our loved ones or, if we are carers for the terminally ill, for our patients and clients, all the discussions about whether near death experiences are real or not become somewhat irrelevant. There is no need to take sides in a debate but rather to allow that, whether 'real' or not, these experiences form part of the normal and natural part of the dying process. Being able to validate the experiences in this way, or even the idea that such experiences may occur, can allow the dying person and their family and friends permission to trust their own instincts and ideas, which even if not scientifically verifiable, are undoubtedly as real as any other belief we may choose about what is essentially the most profound mystery of life, that all that lives will die. We do not and cannot know the meaning of this beyond the purely mundane position taken by scientific and existential thought, except in relation with the experience of a dying person. In earthly matters we trust those who have experience over those who just talk about some things they do not know. Why should it be any less so in understanding about death from those nearest the experience, not despite but because of its unsolvable mystery?

✳

Replacement and Renewal

Reflection

Either in reality or in your imagination:

Reflect on this: if you stand in a meadow at the edge of a hillside and look around you, almost everything you can catch sight of is in a process of dying.

Many of all the living things in your vision will be dead long before you are. New plants, new living beings, some already growing unnoticed, will replace them.

Now consider: if not for this constant process of replacement and renewal, there would be no living things to view.

Freedom

Reflection

Relax and centre...Think about *Freedom*. Hold the concept of Freedom in your mind and reflect upon it. Ask yourself questions about this quality: what is it? What is its nature? What is its meaning? and so on.

Be still. Do not think about Freedom any more, just be receptive; what does Freedom mean to you now?

Realise the value of Freedom, its purpose, and its use in your life and on the planet as a whole. What differences would there be if Freedom were in abundance?

Desire Freedom.

Allow Freedom to be in your body, assume a posture that expresses this quality. Relax all your tensions and let them drift away. Breathe slowly.

Allow Freedom to express itself on your face. Visualise yourself with that expression.

Evoke the quality of Freedom. Imagine you are in a place where you feel Freedom; a quiet beach, with a loved one, in the middle of a crowded city, in a temple of Freedom, wherever you choose. Try to really feel it.

Repeat the word Freedom several times. Let the quality permeate you, to the point of identification if possible. Allow yourself to be Freedom.

Resolve to remain infused with Freedom, to be the living embodiment of Freedom, to radiate Freedom.

Whenever you feel down or disconnected, recall within yourself this feeling of Freedom

PART 4

LIFE AGAIN

"Only when they are awake do they begin to know
they dreamed. Then comes the great awakening,
when we find out that life itself is a great dream."

Chuang Tzu [49]

All a Dream

A re you awake? This may not seem so obvious as at first appears. Sometimes during dreams we have experiences where, as far as we know, we appear to be awake. What if the whole of life were just such a dream? What if we could awaken ourselves so that we felt better and more engaged with our life – and our death?

If we are going to awaken ourselves to the fact that in our everyday life we may be living within a dream, we have to find ways to 'check out reality' and see if we are dreaming or not. The famous 'pinch me to see if I am dreaming' is not so silly: if you check yourself out that way, if the pinch doesn't hurt, you know you are in a dream. This opens up the possibility of becoming lucid – that is, awakening within a dream. In our so-called 'waking' life we can perform many such 'reality checks' throughout the day, thus reminding ourselves that we are in a dream: thus, we may awaken within 'this dream' too. This is the famous 'waking state' in many of the mystery schools of both the East and West. Such reality checks include asking: 'Am I dreaming?' and 'Who is dreaming?' then to do something to check if it is so or not. If you try to fly for instance, you know whether you are awake in this dream or not! Whilst requiring great will and imagination, a simple and effective practice is constantly trying to recall and remind ourselves that whatever we are doing, we are in a dream.

The quote from Chuang Tzu opposite suggests a certainty about what is waking and what is dreaming, but the famous story from his life involves him expressing the more realistic situation of not knowing one way or the other. The essence of the story is that Chuang Tzu wakes up one day having had a dream of being a butterfly and realizes that he doesn't know whether he is a man who has just had a dream of being a butterfly, or if he is a butterfly now having the dream of being a man. When we are honest with ourselves, we realize this is our true human condition. Rather than limiting us, this uncertainty actually liberates us.

If we can awaken from the 'dream' or trance of life, where we are not as fully awake as we may at first imagine, consider how this may apply to our perceptions of death. If as Chuang-tzu says, life is all a great dream, might not death be the great awakening?

*

Not Really Here

What if we are not really here? How can we consider death and rebirth if we haven't fully incarnated, or fully been born, in the first place? The ancient tradition of Kabbalah[50] offers an interesting perspective on death and rebirth which says basically that before we can die and be reborn we have to be here in the first place. At first that can sound strange, but when you think about it, are you here – are you sure? Kabbalists[51] believe that we live our lives not fully incarnated and, indeed, our real task in being alive is to bring ourselves fully to earth. Following the maxim 'as above so below'[52], the notion is that until you are 'fully here' you are incomplete. So, how do Kabbalists suggest we bring ourselves fully into incarnation? Two ways: by simply being here now (of course, not as simple as it sounds) incarnated into your body, and secondly through finding and living from your heart centre as opposed to centering your life experience on your genitals or belly (that is, sex and food!) both of which are more common positions to centre on than the heart.[53]

We have two choices or possibilities: to not notice, to live life as if it is 'all real', or to develop a sense of self, an awareness of one's own consciousness. We then need the self awareness and will to take that final step into full consciousness. To understand this more fully, we have to go back to creation, to the source of everything. The 'source'[54] (or whatever we are created from) created us as a perfect reflection (in 'his' own image as it says in the Bible), so by definition we therefore must have the self-awareness and choice possibilities that our creator has.

We have become separated and we deal with this separation through creating our illusionary world where we imagine we are here but in fact we have never fully realised our potential as independent living creatures. For Christian Kabbalists[55], Jesus is an example of what it means to fully come to earth: it is to identify so fully with your heart that even to be tortured and crucified (or in our cases to fully feel the pain of being incarnate) is a key to the final step of being here so fully we are ready to transcend the duality of both pleasure and pain.

The Kabbalistic notion is that the creator or source – whatever that is – created everything (each of us and all living beings) in order to get to know itself. Then the creator realised its creation (in its own image) was – as it were – too perfect, so created a barrier to separate the created – us – from the creator. This is the basis of the Genesis story, implying that the challenge of life is to get to know ourselves so we fully reflect and by implication take on the wisdom and understanding of our creator.

So Kabbalists claim that we don't fully incarnate to earth but remain in an imaginary realm, an illusion that we believe we are fully here when we are not. Death and rebirth come into the picture when we consider our options in this philosophy. The first option is to remain on the wheel of death/rebirth, to continue in the general pool of consciousness, with any sense of individuality a passing illusion. The second option is to bring ourselves fully to earth, fully incarnated and thus open up a channel to our own heart energy, the centre of individual consciousness. Then when we die we are reborn with a continuity of consciousness albeit not necessarily consciously remembered in any specific life.

As with Buddhism, however, it is probably best to consider reincarnation as a temporary measure, a step or series of steps on the way to the final goal of re-joining with the oneness of everything, being 'one with god'. Then death and rebirth are seen as not only about successive incarnations (in this life or another) but an ongoing process in which we die and are reborn each moment.

The question then changes from: 'what if we are not really here' to the more pertinent question: 'what if we are really here, really, not in an illusion or dream of a waking state, but truly awake?' Then we live in paradise and are surrounded by abundance in both the twin poles of life and death, themselves seen for what they are, changes in the continuous consciousness of self.

*

Through the Stages

Elisabeth Kubler-Ross[56], a Swiss psychologist, discovered through her work that many dying people are comforted if someone is willing to listen openly to their expressed fears and fantasies. The vast majority of dying people, she also discovered, once over the initial shock of learning their condition, go through five psychological stages:

• denial
• anger
• bargaining
• grieving
• acceptance.

In the denial stage, the individual refuses to recognize reality and acts as if the condition does not exist. They may then become angry, resenting that others enjoy good health and blaming doctors and relatives for their inability to help. The bargaining stage follows: trying to 'buy time' often through prayers or in return for being a better person. This stage is followed by a true recognition of the reality of their situation. The person enters the stage of grief and depression, mourning the loss of his or her own life. When the final stage of acceptance is reached, the person may still be angry and fearful but is now prepared to die with peace and dignity.

Perhaps if we consider how we go through these stages when confronted with a difficult transition in life, and the choices available to us when we become conscious of this pattern, we may prepare ourselves to confront death with a greater awareness and with dignity. We do this not through denying any of the stages but through accepting them as a natural response to such a transition.

✳

Life Concerns

Existential Psychology[57] identifies four major concerns in life: death, freedom, relationship and meaning. Different conflicts arise from each of these issues: for instance, fear of ageing and dying, feelings of confinement and isolation, burn out, and meaninglessness. With all of these concerns, it can help to identify how these issues affect you as an individual and in relationship to others. Contemplate and look deeper into the meaning within how these issues are experienced, and find a new, happier and more joyful perspective on the unfolding events of life. Our concern here is death and dying and its associated effects on us. Death is, after all, the obvious ultimate concern: however full of life we may be now, we are certain that one day we will cease to exist. There is no escape from death, and, if not fully consciously then certainly unconsciously, we respond with mortal terror. The existential conflict created within us is between this awareness of the inevitability of death and our natural wish to continue to be.

This   segues   with   the   issue   of   meaning   and meaninglessness of our lives. If we must die, each ultimately alone in an indifferent universe, then what meaning does life have? Why do we live – and, practically, how shall we live? We each have to construct our own meaning in life yet can a meaning of one's own making be strong enough to enable us to function beyond our deepest inner dread?

One attempt to bring perspective to this situation was formulated by James Bugental[58], a former president of the American Association of Humanistic Psychology.   The basic principles he postulated are intended as an antidote to existential meaninglessness without resorting to the 'invention' of an 'outside creator'. The five postulates are that:

• a human is greater than the sum of his or her parts and cannot be understood from scientific study of any or all the parts;

- a human lives in a human context and cannot be understood without including our interpersonal experience;

- a human is aware and can only be understood when our continuous, many layered self awareness is recognised;

- a human has choice and is not a bystander to existence, each of us individually and collectively together create our own experience; and

- a human is intentional and our existence orientates us to the future which has purpose, potential, value and meaning.

✲

Fear of Dying

Reflect on the following question: at this moment, at the deepest levels of your being, what is it you most deeply dread?

The fear of death haunts us, is a dark unsettling presence at the edge of consciousness. Ego survival depends upon keeping it at bay – ego developed in the first place to protect us from our deep awareness of our temporariness.

Ego is based on the denial of our impermanence and this denial shapes the character structure we develop.[59] So long as we deny that life and death are interdependent and that they exist simultaneously not consecutively, then we deny our wholeness and remain in a partial state held in place by the machinations of ego which, we eventually have to concede, are doomed, for we will die – it is an essential part of life.

Some people, the Stoics[60] for example, have maintained that death is the most important event in life, and St Augustine[61] said: "It is only in the face of death that man's self is born." That truly places death as central to life, or at least to living life to the fullest. There is no life to be found greater or more complete than that which comes along with death. Avoidance of this is inauthentic; we become involved in the idle chatter of everyday world, overly concerned about the way things are rather than how we are. Is it such a big step to marvel not at the way things are but that they are? Maybe not, not in reality, but most of the time we live and act not only as if it is, but as if such a choice is not on offer.

Avoidance of our existential reality and avoidance of the presence of death can take many forms, for instance:
• being special (not me, I won't die)
• being a compulsive hero (I want nothing, I fear nothing, I am free)
• being a workaholic (living is doing, so long as I do I will live)
• being narcissistic (I have an importance that only I can see)

- being aggressive and trying to always be in control (I have the power)
- being anxious (I cannot concern myself with things like death, it is too much for me)
- being a rescuer or server (I might burn out but I am doing good work)
- being in complete denial (it's going to die but I am not)

Spend a while now being mindful, marvelling not at the way things are but that they are.

Meaning or Meaninglessness?

Is there meaning in death? Is life meaningless? Are these two questions the two sides of the same coin? By inquiring into the meaning of life it is as if somehow we are not satisfied with just living life – we need to know what it's for. If we all die and nothing of us endures, then it is hard to find sense and meaning in life. Individually at such times we may enter what has been called the 'crisis of meaning' where a sense of no meaning, no goals, no values lead us into distress. We humans innately wish to acquire meaning and if we cannot, our sense of ourselves crumbles. This is true collectively as well as individually, as can be seen by the crises currently engulfing the planet all of which, in this sense, are crises of meaning.

One way of possibly avoiding this sense of meaninglessness is to apply a cosmic meaning to life. Everything that happens is part of a divine plan. Versions of this divine plan abound and there is nothing to really stop us cherry-picking our preferred options. For instance, we may choose to believe it is our job to ascertain and fulfil God's will or to surrender to it; or we can practice the noble Buddhist precepts to purify ourselves; we can decide to make a particular day holy, and so on. With all this striving for perfection in ourselves, we have to take care to avoid the trap of trying to become the perfect god, for we will always fall short of perfection. Many of our myths and legends involving gods and goddesses highlight their imperfections which can seem only too human. Perhaps we can reach a state of mind where imperfection is perfection and, along with Teilhard de Chardin[62] see in life a cosmic coherence, the unfolding of a play in which each of us has a role to play.

Not that we need religion, or even spiritual inquiry, to attempt to overcome meaninglessness. A secular, personal meaning can be found in many ways, perhaps most effectively through simply accepting life is what it is. That of course is much more difficult than it sounds, but the challenge of striving for it can, in itself, bring meaning to life. Another alternative is to let go of any consideration of meaning and purpose in life and, along with Camus[63], learn to live life 'with dignity in the face of absurdity'.

Jean-Paul Sartre[64] said, 'it is meaningless that we are born, it is meaningless that we die.' Even if that were true, it does not mean we cannot find meaning, cannot discover something to live life for, and something to live life by. And, truth is, like all our ancestors before us, we will continue to ask the question 'what is the meaning of my life? for just in the asking of this question we confer a meaning on life.

If the Existentialists are right and the act of engagement is what at least keeps us from the depression of meaninglessness (there is no suggestion from them that it confers meaning), then this is equally true of death. We can find the meaning in death, in other words, not through avoiding it but through engaging with it. The qualities that Sartre named as being those which probably may alleviate suffering in life were comradeship, action, freedom, rebellion against oppression, service to others, enlightenment, self-realisation, but above all engagement.

There is a big distinction between engaging with the world and turning engagement into a crusade. There's an old expression 'beware a man with a mission' and the history of missionary good-intention turning into fundamentalist zeal is only too well known. Don Johnson[65], the somatic body practitioner, suggests we can all be classified into pilgrims or missionaries: pilgrims engage with the world with an open mind, inquiring into what is, whereas missionaries engage with the world with a set idea of how it should be. The dangers of the 'missionary position' cannot be over-emphasised and are especially relevant in the arena of death. You do always have a choice. To be with someone who is helping you be with what is happening to you is more enriching than to be with someone who is telling you what they think you should believe or how you should act. As Jesus says (in Luke 12:27): 'Consider the lilies in the field, how they grow, they toil not, neither do they spin'.[66]

If we create our own reality then our own attitude to any situation is, by definition, of central importance. You may not necessarily be able to do anything about the condition you are in (internally or externally) but how you respond to it is up to you and you alone. Life changes your body and you still have a choice how to experience it. More than 2000 years ago, Epictetus[67] expressed this perfectly: 'I must die. I must be imprisoned. I must suffer exile. But must I die groaning? Must I whine as well? Can anyone hinder me from going into exile with a smile?'

✳

Life in Death

Of course, no one really wants to think about their own death and yet is is vital we do so otherwise we are simply lulling ourselves into disregarding what is a real and central issue in life. Life cannot exist without death. Our existence is governed by outside forces greater than us but if we ignore them until the fateful moment of our demise then we abrogate our responsibility for ourselves and – worse – we miss the opportunity to know ourselves, to grow, and to find our own meaning in life.

When we engage with our true existential situation – that we will die, there's no choice in this – then we can see how insignificant, on a cosmic scale, the effects of a human life are. That does not mean we have to let go of our personal choices and blindly follow our fate as if we are victims. The truth is that there has always been an unbridgeable chasm between our hopes, desires and aspirations and the demands and necessities of life. This is the inherent tragedy in our existence yet it is also what offers us the grit from which we may find the jewels of understanding that can help us engage truthfully with whatever life throws at us.

Yes, individually we may be unimportant in the greater scheme of things but we still need to inquire into our life's purpose and meaning otherwise life is a repetitive chore to be lived without variation or engagement. The impulse to search for meaning opens us to something else, something that may be entirely ourselves and yet paradoxically contains the something greater than ourselves which can free us from despair and psychic suffering.

Life isn't easy, not if we wish to remain awake and engaged even in the face of our impending cessation. At all stages of life we can become distracted, grow unmindful and even cynical, falling back into a trance of meaninglessness. It behoves us to place our search for meaning at the forefront of life, even at the end of life. Indeed, the imminence of our death may be just what is needed to supply the last key to our understanding of who we really are. Despair then can be seen as a signal to become even more deeply involved (and not doze off); fear, confusion, and hopelessness remind us to continue our quest for meaning not in spite of but because of these difficult emotions. Like a hunter waiting for his prey we then approach death with the fullest awareness possible.

In the final analysis, when we are at death's door, it is not pleasure, wealth or fame, not even the closest of relationships which many say are the last thing of meaning as we approach death, but a life filled by well-being that is our saving grace. Memories of good times from our past may comfort us, but as we are stepping over the threshold, it is our well-being at that very moment that ensures our safe passage. *What we may be*[68] is not something fixed but requires untiring, continuous inquiry.

✴

The Inner Guide

Reflection

Relax and centre yourself. Imagine you are in a meadow where the sun is shining and the birds are singing. Spend some time really feeling your presence in this meadow. Notice what you can hear, what you can see, what you feel.

Explore the meadow, walking in various directions, really feeling your feet on the ground beneath you, taking your time to really enjoy the sights and sensations you experience in your meadow.

Become aware that you are about to meet someone who is inimately involved with the evolution of your life and the presence of death in life. This person is your inner guide – you might see him or her as a wise old person, as a guardian angel, or simply as someone whose eyes express great love and care for you. However you visualise this person, let the image of him or her appear clearly before you in your meadow. Allow yourself to fully experience the excitement and interest such a contact invokes.

You can now engage this being in a dialogue and, in whatever way seems best to you at this time, ask about the issues, questions and choices you currently have in your life. The dialogue may be verbal or non verbal, it may take place on a visual or symbolic level, but however it occurs really relish this time you are spending with your inner guide.

Also ask about your death. Let your inner guide's wisdom and understanding help you realise your connection, your ability to love and your power to relax into whatever experiences come your way. Ask your guide to be with you when you make transitions, especially through the gates of death.

When you are ready, thank your guide for having appeared to you and once more feel your feet firmly placed on the ground. Bring your consciousness back to your surroundings and spend some time considering what you have learned and how you can put this learning into practice in your life.

If you wish to further deepen your connection to your Inner Guide (especially in the form of a 'Guardian Angel') you might like the following guided imagery.

Reflection

Imagine you are in a meadow on a beautiful sunny day. Truly become aware of your environment. Look around you at what you see on this beautiful, sunny day. Listen to birds singing in nearby trees, feel a cool, refreshing breeze caress your cheeks.

Notice how you are dressed, especially what are you wearing on your feet. Feeling your feet on the ground, start walking a little, aware of how you feel on this sunny day.

Look around you and notice what you can see in each direction – there may be trees, distant mountains, hills, and so on. Build up a strong sense of being wherever you are.

Notice that in one direction, just a little distance from you, there is a shining tunnel of light in which you can see a temple, its structure glistening in the bright light … Start walking in the direction of this temple, really being conscious of what you feel as you do so.

Feel the contact of your feet on the ground as you walk towards the temple, looking about you at the trees, the bushes, the grass and flowers.

Use all your senses to fully appreciate where you are Be aware of the scenery, the warmth of the sun on your skin, the scents in the air ... also be aware of your anticipation, excitement, whatever you feel as you walk towards your temple.

You are now approaching your temple. See your temple, in whatever form it has appeared to you, as bathed in clear, vibrant light.

You will soon enter this temple, but before you do so be aware that when you do you will be surrounded by silence and safety.

Walk up to the entrance of the temple and step inside. You feel the atmosphere around you, the peace and silence, the vibrant splendour of this temple. Spend as much time as you wish exploring the inside of the temple.

Notice that in the centre of the temple is an altar. As you approach this altar you see that something is on it which catches your eye and draws your attention. As you reach the altar you see it is a crown. Imagine this crown now in whatever form it appears to you.

As you stand silently before the altar, a ray of sunlight shines brightly onto the crown. The crown is for you to wear. Lift it from the altar and place it on your head ... As you do so, take time to really feel your body connecting strongly with your inner divinity, being infused with healing energy.

Silently stand before the altar as sunlight breaks through window and shines brightly on your body, feeling yourself filled with warming healing energy of sunlight.

You sense with all your being that you are now in the presence of your guardian angel ... Really feel the presence of your angel, alert and alive as you silently contemplate your experience in the light in your temple.

If you wish you may specifically ask your angel to be with you throughout your life, and to guide you beyond the confines of life and death when seen as opposites.

Still wearing the crown, you turn around and see that your angel has silently placed a robe on the floor behind you, a robe that symbolises silence and protection. Before leaving the temple, you pick up the robe and wrap it around you.

The time has come to leave the temple ... In whatever way feels right to you, thank the forces and energies of this temple for your gifts and in your own time, turn and leave.

Once outside, open yourself to the impact of the day, feel a gentle breeze on your cheeks and listen to the singing of birds.

When you are ready, fairly rapidly, with ease and a light spring in your step, return to where you started your journey. Open your eyes and, in your own time, come back to the everyday world. Be aware of the blessings in embodying a life that encompasses both living and dying.

Make sure you have fully brought yourself out of this experience, aware that your temple, your robe and your crown are always available to you, whatever your circumstances.

✳

Entering Silence

I quoted the poet Andrew Marvell near the beginning of this book, that 'the grave is a fine and private place but none, I think, do there embrace.' Marvell wrote these words hundreds of years ago and they still have a ring of truth about them. What if we look at this from inside rather than outside, however, and find that there is something to embrace inside the grave, in the afterlife, and that is complete and utter silence. Complete and utter silence – words with a ring to them: complete and utter silence – it doesn't sound all that bad, does it?

Total inner silence is the goal of many inner traditions and many different techniques have been devised to help an individual reach such a state. These include: various forms of meditation; various visualisation methods; using sound to block out the chatter of the inner dialogue; a variety of movement exercises; yoga and breathing techniques; and inducing intense excitement. All of these methods aim to stop our incessant inner thought processes which, when stopped, allow us to access a different dimension beyond time, a dimension of total freedom from the concerns of the duality of life and death.

Inner silence is not just about the absence of sound but involves a deep connection with an immensely powerful energy that transcends both sound and silence. This energy is your essential self, or quite simply, your essence. When you empty your mind there is the space for this energy to appear. Trying to connect with your essence without stopping the chatter of your inner dialogue with yourself has been likened to stirring up water to look for the moon, rather than stilling the water so it becomes a mirror in which you can see a reflection of your innermost essence.

✳

Reflections

The following meditations adapted from the Zenrin[69] help you focus on being exactly who you are at exactly this moment. Try them out, you may be surprised not only how centring these suggestions can be, but also how comforting.

✳

Look at an object, then slowly withdraw your sight from it, then slowly withdraw your thought from it, then enter silence.

✳

Look attentively at an object. Do not go on to another object. Here, in the middle of this object – the silence.

✳

Feel the presence of an object as your own consciousness, and leaving behind concern for self, enter the silence.

✳

Wherever your attention alights on an object, at this very point, the silence.

✳

See as if for the first time an object, and at that moment, enter the silence.

✳

Wherever your mind is wandering, internally or externally, at this very place, silence.

*

Consider the entire area of your present form as limitlessly spacious and silent.

*

Just as you have the impulse to do something, stop and enter silence.

*

Feel your substance, bones, flesh, blood, all saturated with inner silence.

*

Feel yourself as pervading all directions, far and near, and then the silence.

*

As breath turns from down to up, and again as breath comes from up to down, through both these turns, realize and enter silence.

*

Last Words

No one can really have the last word on death, but I think these three philosophers – Marx, Morecombe and Sinatra[70] – were on the right track with their final words.

"Go on, get out!
Last words are for fools who haven't said enough!"

Karl Marx, asked by his housekeeper for his last words

"I'm glad that's over"

Eric Morecombe, just before dying after his last stage performance

"The best is yet to come"

Frank Sinatra

✳

NOTES

1   Quoted by Robert Anton Wilson in *Email to the Universe*
    (New Falcon, USA 2005). Robert Anton Wilson (1932-2007)
    was a relativist, magician and engaging writer whose work
    explores the myths and fables of our modern age with both
    insight and humour. In *Cosmic Trigger* (And/Or, USA 1977)
    Wilson claims to reveal 'the final secret' of enlightened be-
    ings when in answering the question 'what do you do when
    somebody keeps giving you negative energy?' he replies:
    'Come back with all the positive energy you have.' The con-
    cept that what you give out returns to you is central to this
    philosophy, and to keep to this tenet in the face of negativity
    is the most profound act a human can perform. It is a more
    active way of understanding the more passively phrased in-
    junction from Christianity to 'turn the other cheek.'

2   From 'To His Coy Mistress' by Andrew Marvell (1621-1681).
    Marvell was a metaphysical poet, romantic and, in later life,
    a politician. The poem, on one level a seduction attempt,
    deeply touches into our existential reality and reveals a soul-
    ful heart, as do many of Marvell's poems. The poem ends:
    Now let us sport us while we may;
    And now, like amorous birds of prey,
    Rather at once our time devour,
    Than languish in his slow-chapt power.
    Let us roll all our strength, and all
    Our sweetness, up into one ball:
    And tear our pleasures with rough strife,
    Through the iron gates of life.
    Thus, though we cannot make our Sun
    Stand still, yet we will make him run.

3   Research suggests that more than a quarter of Americans and
    an even larger number of Europeans believe that reincarna-
    tion is possible (even if they apparently belong to religions
    that teach otherwise.) Put those figures together with all the
    adherents to religions that do teach reincarnation and you'll

see how I came to assert this. Not that exactly how many people believe in one thing compared to another is that important; and even if as a sceptic you were to say that the migration of souls is a comforting fantasy to avoid facing the reality of death, it is still a remarkably large number of us who believe in this possibility.

4 To all those who believe in the teachings of religions such as Christianity and Islam, add all those who believe in the versions of reincarnation that include karmic consequence (i.e. you reap in future lives what you sow in this one.) As the adage that your actions have consequences seems to be true in life, then if reincarnation is true perhaps there is something to be said for this notion – so long as we stay clear of literalistic interpretations (heaven a beautiful garden and hell a pit of raging fire, for instance.)

5 If we achieve the 'right' level of consciousness, according to, for instance, some interpretations of Buddhism, rather than return to life on the wheel of fortune we will merge with the Oneness from whence we originally emerged and transcend all duality and desire. So long as it doesn't become a way of avoiding reality, a back-to-the-womb type of activity, then this possibility may spur us to reflection, contemplation and/or meditation, all of which can serve us in this life well enough without concerning ourselves as to whether it may gain us 'brownie points' in a cosmic hierarchy.

6 Surprise is the emotion which is not only a response to change but which in itself can bring about change and, approached actively, can reduce some of the anxieties associated with death. How lovely a surprise each moment can be if we look at life (and death) this way.

7 Our bodies replace about 1% of their cells every day which means 1% of your body is new today and another 1% tomorrow, meaning you get a new body every ninety days! That's a pretty close estimate if not entirely accurate. Your skin, your body, your organs, your tissues, your heart – every part of

a body is constantly in a state of regeneration. Our eyes are replaced approximately every forty-eight hours. It is curious then that eye conditions such as myopia are passed on from one generation of cells to another, or for instance a heart problem is not regenerated away as the cells replace themselves, but it does at least give us the possibility, through changing the messages our brain sends to the cells, of curing certain ailments or, at the very least, recognizing that there is something in us that is beyond any particular condition from which we suffer.

8   Julius Henry Marx (1890-1977), better known as Groucho Marx, was the American comedian and actor famous for his work in the Marx Brothers comedy team. He was a master of the unusual and unexpected retort and his last words, as quoted here, are typical of his humour. What better way to face the approach of death than with humour?

9   It isn't much of a tradition if it doesn't include teachings on how to approach and face death and, most importantly, how to live with the knowledge of the presence of death throughout life. Whilst some religions stress comforting (and for the 'uninitiated', not so comforting) ideas of what might await us after death, the inner traditions stress the importance of being fully in life, living with the presence of death and transmuting it into something positive rather than negative.

10   ADEs (after-death experiences) are sometimes distinguished from NDEs (near-death experiences) although the features are somewhat the same or similar. Common amongst ADE experiences is the idea that the individual realises themselves as an infinite being (who had previously existed within a human body but was more than that body.) In this view, we are so identified with the body in life we 'forget' our divine and immortal self as an entity separate from our physical, human incarnation. The body is then often seen as a vehicle for life experience, to be lived in to the full and let go of when the time comes to move back to one's true inner self or centre.

11 Plato (428-437 BCE) was an ancient Greek philosopher, the second of the great trio of ancient Greeks – following Socrates and preceding Aristotle – who between them laid the philosophical foundations of Western culture. Plato was also a mathematician, writer of intense dialogues, and founder of the Academy in Athens, the first institution of higher learning in the Western world. Plato's idea that what we experience through our senses is at odds with common sense presages theories of modern physics that similarly transcend 'common sense'. According to Plato, physical objects and physical events are 'shadows' of their ideal or perfect forms, and exist only to the extent that they mirror on a lower plane archetypal versions of themselves that exist on higher (or deeper) planes. Just as shadows are temporary, all physical objects are themselves fleeting phenomena caused by more substantial causes. This is worth reflecting on most deeply for, if it is true (and for all we really know, it might be) it completely changes our relationship with death which may then be the experience through which we come back to the knowledge of the true meaning of existence.

12 This is where karma and reincarnation come together. Vedanta, the philosophy underlying all the different Hindu faiths, makes one of the interesting arguments for this position. Not only our actions but also our thoughts create impressions in both our minds and in the world around us. Christianity teaches that what you sow so do you reap – this is the same message, that all these impressions you make on the universe come back to you – in other words, good thoughts and action create good effects, bad thoughts and actions bad effects. We know this makes sense because we experience it throughout our lives. Vedanta argues that when a person dies, the mind, which contains all a person's mental impressions, continues and migrates into a new physical body (at some point, not necessarily straight away because it doesn't exist in the same linear time frame as us.) It is then useful to consider that if we have created the life we are leading today through our own previous thoughts and actions, we also have the power to create our future life and death (and if you believe it, affect

our future lives.) Especially as we approach death, to know that every thought and action builds our future experience can empower our relationship with our fate.

13   Jean-Paul Sartre (1905-1980) was a French existentialist who became a leading figure in 20th century philosophy. Perhaps the most famous existentialist, Jean-Paul Sartre is often quoted as saying that God does not exist, that humans don't have any other choice than to take in hand their destiny through the political and social conditions under which they exist. He didn't actually say God doesn't exist but rather that even if God did exist, that would change nothing. On a more personal level he suggested that life has no meaning the moment you lose the illusion of being eternal. So engage with what is.

14   When Joni Mitchell sang 'We are golden, we are stardust...' in her 1960's song 'Woodstock' she was scientifically correct: all the elements on earth – except the very lightest – were created in the heart of a massive star. Gold, one of our most precious elements, comes from a supernova explosion at the end of such a star's life. The iron in our blood and the calcium in our bones – all the elements that make us up – come from distant space. In other words, something of you has been – and will be – around for a very, very long time.

15   To experience this we don't even have to concern ourselves with concepts like 'soul' as the following meditation from Psychosynthesis clearly shows.

Consider this: Your body may find itself in different conditions of health or sickness, it may be rested or tired, but however you experience it, there is a 'you' that, because it experiences your body, must be more than just your body. You can truly say: 'I have a body and I am more than my body.' You treat it well, you seek to keep it in good health, but it is not you, yourself.

   Similarly with your feelings and emotions which are ever-changing, sometimes in contradictory ways. They may swing from love to hatred, from calm to anger, from joy to sorrow; a wave of anger may temporarily submerge you, and you know that in time it will pass, therefore you are not this anger. Since you can observe and understand your feelings, it is clear that they are not your self. You can truly say: 'I have feelings, and I am more than my feelings'.

Your mind is a valuable tool of discovery and expression, but it is not the essence of your being either. Its contents are constantly changing as it embraces new ideas, knowledge, and experience, and makes new connections. Sometimes your thoughts seem to be independent of you and if you try to control them they seem to refuse to obey you. Therefore your thoughts cannot be you, your self. You can then say: 'I have a mind and I am more than my mind.'

Being more than your body, your feelings, and your mind, you can recognise that you are a centre of consciousness capable of observing, directing and using all your psychological processes and your physical body. You can say: ' I am a centre of pure self-consciousness and of will' and realise this as an experienced fact in your awareness.

16 Individuation is a concept that appears in numerous fields but here particularly as used in psychology and by Carl Jung. In very general terms, it describes the process whereby the undifferentiated newborn gradually tends to become more individual as he or she progresses through life up to a point (after leaving home, psychologically rather than physically) where the differentiated components of that person tend toward becoming a more indivisible whole thus conferring a sense of being 'one's very own self'.

17 Remember when you meet the term 'reflection' in this book it indicates that the following section, whilst it may simply be read, can also be used as an exercise in mindful self-inquiry. There's a section How To Use This Book at the beginning of the book. I think you'll find that if you are the sort of person who doesn't do exercises in books, if you at least read them through you'll find these reflections will have an effect.

18 Mindfulness means to be intentionally aware of your thoughts and actions in the present moment and to remain non-judgmental of whatever you encounter in your body, thoughts and feelings. An excellent description of how to do it comes from Tich Nhat Hanh: 'While practicing mindfulness, don't be dominated by the distinction between good and evil, thus creating a battle within oneself... Whenever a wholesome thought arises, acknowledge it: "A wholesome thought has just arisen." If an unwholesome thought arises, acknowledge it as well: "An unwholesome thought has just arisen." Don't dwell on it or try to get rid of it. To acknowledge it is enough. If they are still there, acknowledge they are still there. If they have gone, acknowledge they have gone. That way the practitioner is able to hold his mind and to obtain the mindfulness of the mind.'

19 This riddle probably does not originate with the Oedipus story but is a later add-on of an old riddle that predates the Greek myth. In the Oedipus story it is used to suggest he is mindful and able to solve problems and mysteries that of course are central to his own story. The riddle asks us to use our minds; in a fragment of Euripides' lost 'Oedipus' he indicates the point of the riddle: 'The mind is what one must consider, the mind. What is the use of physical beauty, when one does not have beauty in the mind?'

20 Thomas Hanna (1928-1990) was a philosopher and body worker who developed Somatics, a powerful approach to mind/body integration. Somatics teaches that, through improving our control from within, we can learn to recapture our freedom of movement and physical comfort. The key to this recovery is the brain understood as a master control center for our muscles (not through 'thinking' but rather through making real connections between the brain and movement.) Through somatic exercises you can potentially regain freedom of movement and physical comfort. Recommended reading: *Somatics* by Thomas Hanna (Da Capo, USA, 1988) and all books on this subject by Don Hanlon Johnson.

21 This powerful quote and all these from Thomas Hanna are
    from Somatics, q.v.

22 As of writing this note on the 17th October 2007, the world
    population stands at 6,753,716,440 and increasing by 3 indi-
    viduals every second or so. I wrote 6 billion in the text but as
    you can see we are edging up towards 7 billion. Is it a com-
    forting thought that more people are born than are dying?

23 Perhaps inevitably, more not less people are born than die
    each year. Recent estimates put the number of people dying
    each year between 50 and 80 million whilst the number of
    new born babies is between 120 and 140 million. That's a lot
    of new mouths to feed each year (and as we all know only
    too well, a lot of them will not be fed sufficiently or, in the
    worst places, not at all.)

24 You can find estimated life span figures for lots of other crea-
    tures on the internet. Of course, the actual life span will be
    shortened, sometimes considerably, depending on various
    environmental factors, where diet is poor and so on. Humans
    sometimes play a major role in this, too, often rather shock-
    ingly. Whereas a cow might expect twenty or more years of
    life, a member of a milking herd in the U.K. may only be kept
    alive for two to three years before going to slaughter. At one
    tenth of its potential life, it is equivalent to a human child be-
    ing put to forced labour and then killed at around eight years
    of age. I know it's different, but it is a salutary thought.

25 Fritz Perls (1893-1970), was the German-born founder of Ge-
    stalt Therapy which he devised with his wife Laura in the
    1940s. Gestalt therapy promotes awareness along with a fo-
    cus on the unity of all present experiences and feelings, and
    an understanding of the contact between oneself and the en-
    vironment. The 'gestalt prayer' devised by Perls as a sum-
    mary of its principles, is very useful to help put difficulties in
    relationship into perspective.
    "I am I and you are you.
    I am not in this world to live up to your expectations,

And you are not in this world to live up to mine.
You are you, and I am I, and if by chance we find each other,
it's beautiful.
If not, that is alright too."
You might like to try sharing this with someone close to you,
saying the prayer to one another a line at a time. Don't forget the last line which is important if you want the prayer to
have the fullest impact.

26 Contemplation on death is considered very important in
Buddhism because by recognising how short life is we are
most likely to live it fully and, through familiarizing ourselves with the death process, we remove the fear at the time
of death. This part of this meditation is based on some Buddhist practices that ask us to reflect on 'difficult' deaths – the
more you face horrible circumstances the less you may fear
them. Traditionally, in Buddhist countries, people are also
encouraged to go to a burial ground or cemetery to contemplate death and familiarize themselves with this inevitable
event. If you have a chance, that's not a bad idea.

27 Tarot cards are pictorial, symbolic representations of the cycles of time, and the processes we go through in connecting
and interacting with these cycles of time. Tarot can help us
understand our own essential nature, how we live in cycles
within cycles, and how to understand our relationships with
other beings, indeed with all life. That everything changes is
the only certainty in our lives, and the tarot is a sophisticated
tool, not for showing us what will be, but for reflecting on
what is and revealing the possibilities of what might be.

28 Or, more simply, as we move from birth through youth to
adulthood we are separating ourselves from what has gone
before (being in the womb, being a child, being a member of
our family of birth etc.) and making our own way in life, creating an identity for ourselves (this is what is termed 'individuation' or sometimes 'differentiation'.) At the same time
we inevitably become attached to, or identified with, aspects
of this identity we create. As we get older, and hopefully ma-

ture, we realize that this identity (what I call 'me') is rather more impermanent than we used to think, so we become less identified with it, and this enables us to integrate back towards the oneness from which we originally emerged.

29 Birth is usually expected to be a joyful event, not a sad one, especially by the parents-to-be. We do not really expect a baby to die and as well as intense grief it may bring us face-to-face with our own mortality. Even the idea of a baby dying can be enough to shake off any complacency we may have around death. Think about it.

30 So when we return to the oneness, the complete purity represented by the Fool in the tarot cards, we may ask what was the point of the journey if we simply return to where we started. What is different is that the individual having made this journey now has the experience. Is an atom of hydrogen, once a gas, then combined with oxygen to make water, then separated again to be an atom of hydrogen exactly the same as it was before, or has the 'experience' of being water made a difference? Physically, it would be hard to discover a difference but 'energetically', it is changed through its experience. Of course, that is metaphysical and cannot be proved by science; but think about it: has your experience through life made a difference to whom you were when you started out? Will you be the same when you die as you were when you were born?

31 Kahlil Gibran (1883-1931) was born in what is now Lebanon but spent much of his life in the USA. From obscure beginnings, he became an accomplished artist and writer, most well-known for his book *The Prophet* from which this quote is taken. If you haven't read it, I highly recommend it as one of the most inspiring books ever written. It is composed of twenty six essays in which a wise man discusses the human condition with a group of people. Whilst the quote here concerning death is most appropriate for this book, I could have quoted many other passages from *The Prophet* which express themes relevant to this book. One of my favourite quotes

from Gibran is:
'Your children are not your children.
They are the sons and daughters of Life's longing for itself.
They come through you but not from you,
And though they are with you, yet they belong not to you.
You may give them your love but not your thoughts.
For they have their own thoughts.
You may house their bodies but not their souls,
For their souls dwell in the house of tomorrow, which you cannot
visit, not even in your dreams.'

32 Terri Schiavo (1963 – 2005), was an American woman who
suffered serious brain damage and became dependent on a
feeding tube which led to fifteen years in a persistent vegetative state. Her husband petitioned the court to remove her
feeding tube whilst her parents opposed this, arguing she
was conscious. A prolonged court battle stretched on for sev-
en years and resulted in extensive international media cov-
erage. She died at her hospice in 2005, at the age of 41. Her
parents and husband had still not found agreement.

33 A heart-warming tale but it does bring up serious questions
about how 'alive' or not someone might be when apparently
in a coma or 'brain-dead'. Also, it is quite a salutary tale when
we consider that most people don't recover their energy before dying in this way, reminding us of how important it is to
say our farewells whilst we still have a chance. It would be
rather morbid to take this to its (il-)logical conclusion – that
we should say goodbye to everyone right now in case we die
the next moment – but it might help us to treat other people
better if we consider that each interaction might be the last
with them.

34 The four (or sometimes five) elements of the wise were used
by many ancient philosophies to explain patterns in nature.
It is believed that everything is composed of one or more of
these elements in combination. 'Water', as an element in this
sense, therefore, does not mean H_2O, the substance we drink,
but an abstract idea that exists everywhere and out of which

everything is partly composed. The metal iron, for instance, is ductible (i.e. capable of being drawn out or stretched) because of its watery aspect; its fiery aspect is its magnetic properties; it's conductivity is airy; and it's weight and harness its earthy aspect.

The elements of the wise can also be used in combination, so for instance, we might consider the fiery part of water, the earthy aspect of air and so on. Regarding natural phenomena, then, fire of water is rain, water of water is sea, air of water is gales, earth of water a river; fire of earth is mountains; water of earth is a seashore; air of earth is fields and earth of earth is rocks and caves. It is an interesting and illuminating activity to reflect on aspects of your life and of what elements in what combination they are composed.

35 Exposure of the body to carrion birds such as crows and vultures is not the only method used by Tibetans who also use cremation and, in the case of important monks, preservation techniques. When exposure burial is used, the deceased's body is attended to by monks or qualified 'corpse cutters' who chant and read from the Tibetan Book of the Dead as the body is prepared, then the body is taken to the cremation ground where it will be exposed to the elements. It is tied to a stake and undressed and then the corpse cutters throw pieces of flesh and bone, pounded up and mixed with meal, to the carrion birds.

36 Thanatology is the branch of science that studies death, especially its social and psychological aspects, including the circumstances surrounding a person's death, the grief experienced by the deceased's loved ones, and larger social attitudes towards death. Thanatology is not so concerned, as we are in this book, with the meaning of life and death. Scientifically such concerns are considered irrelevant, and some medical texts refer to inquiries into the meaning of life and death as absurd and futile. Thanatology explores how the questions about the meaning of death affect those involved, not the question itself.

37 Of course this is a very approximate figure but it is no less relevant to reflect on its deep meaning, however abstract it may be, until one of those 'twenty people per minute' is someone you know – or someone you love – or yourself.

38 Stanley Keleman is a practitioner of his own brand of somatic therapy that he has been developing for over thirty-five years. He is a pioneer in the study of the body and its connection to the sexual, emotional, psychological and imaginative aspects of human experience. His book *Living Your Dying* is particularly relevant to our present interest.

39 Stephen Levine is a spiritual teacher and poet, who with his wife, Ondrea, has worked with the dying and their loved ones for many years. Levine is an acknowledged expert in the field and has several best-selling books, all of which I would recommend, especially *Healing into Life and Death* and *Who Dies?* from where this quote is adapted. Levine's focus on being fully alive and exploring the nature of what it is that dies in us is congruent with the intent of this book.

40 Timothy Leary (1920-1996) was a controversial American writer, psychologist and pioneer in psychedelic drug research and use. He became famous as a 1960's counter-culture icon, promoting the use of LSD for therapeutic and spiritual liberation, and popularizing his catch phrase: 'turn on, tune in, drop out.' Far from being the 'mad man' as he was often portrayed in the media, Leary was a genius and true polymath and his book *Design For Dying* is both informative and moving, as it was written soon before his death so is experientially alive with the issues. Timothy Leary was one of the earliest people to choose a particularly modern form of burial – his ashes were sent into space.

41 Thich Nhat Hanh is a Vietnamese Zen Buddhist monk, teacher, author, and peace activist who was nominated for the Nobel Peace Prize by no less than Martin Luther King. His teachings and practices are designed to appeal to people from any religious, spiritual, and political background, being

based on a practice of mindfulness that is adapted to Western cultures. He runs a monastery and spiritual practice centre in France called Plum Village. The quote here is one of many you can find in his books and on the internet that resonate with a deep truth and an even deeper compassion. One of my favourite quotes, from *Touching Peace* is: 'The miracle is not to walk on water. The miracle is to walk on the green earth in the present moment, to appreciate the peace and beauty that are available now.'

42 These may seem like strange questions but they are well worth a little contemplation. If you are not your body, or more than just your body, then you have every reason to believe your existence is beyond the confines of just this life (whatever else you may believe.) If you only exist because you have a body then without a body there would be no you, but your component parts will not cease to exist just because 'you' do. Personally I find it most useful to consider 'I am a body and I am more than a body' because that leaves open the possibility this is true without in any way denying that I am a body, too.

43 Different Christian sects have different views on this notion (technically the issue of 'justification'). St Paul was clear in presenting the view that faith alone is what counts and no amount of good works will ensure someone's place in heaven if their faith is lacking. To depend upon the 'grace' of God to be saved might suggest that it doesn't really matter what you do in life, but that also would involve this God not paying any attention to what you do, which would put God in a strangely remote position. Perhaps in this context it is wise to 'hedge your bets' as it were, and trust in your faith being enough to incur God's grace and do good works just in case (not as outrageous a suggestion as it might first appear since this is the line taken by many Christians themselves.) Perhaps we would do well to remember Jesus' words from the Gospel of Luke: 'you are the ones who justify yourselves in the eyes of men, but God knows your hearts.'

44 Mother Theresa (1910-1997) was an Albanian Catholic nun who founded the Missionaries of Charity and for over forty years worked with and ministered to the poor, sick and dying in Calcutta in India. She was already internationally famous when in 1979 she won the Nobel Peace Prize, and after her death she was beatified by Pope John Paul II. Recent publication of her private letters has shown how through all of her adult life she was plagued by doubts about her faith yet she continued to believe that faith is enough and never let her concerns and doubts interfere with her good work, thus transcending all of the ecclesiastical debates about justification and so on (see last note.) Truly a Saint!

45 Universalists follow a theology that holds all persons and creatures are part of (or at least related to) the divine and will be reconciled to God. Universalism therefore tends towards the acceptance of all religions in an inclusive manner, believing in an inevitable reconciliation between humanity and the divine.

46 Jehovah's Witnesses are generally quite unpopular when they call at people's houses uninvited, but if one takes the time to talk to the individuals doing this they are often kind and considerate people. Jehovah's Witnesses are members of an international religious group who believe they practice a restored form of first-century Christianity governed by their understanding of scriptural laws and principles from the Bible. Their religion was developed in response to what they saw as compromise and corruption in mainstream Christianity and they dispute many of the doctrines in the mainstream Christian religions (such as the Trinity and the immortality of the soul.) As they believe Armageddon is imminent they spend as much time as they can preaching their message – that the wicked will be destroyed, and survivors, along with millions of others who will be resurrected, will form a new society of immortals living in an earthly paradise ruled by God.

47 The modern 'folk belief' that Quantum physics 'proves' that the mind of the observer of an experiment affects the results is not entirely supportable except in so far as we all 'know' through our experience how much what we think affects everything around us. It would be very satisfying if modern science would fully support this notion but it is not so as many scientists dispute any such claims. Indeed, the issue of the relationship between mind and body has existed over many centuries and various monistic and dualistic theories have been proposed to explain this connection. At our current state of scientific understanding, we may suspect that quantum mechanics and consciousness are related, but the details are not at all clear. In early interpretations of quantum mechanics it seemed that understanding apparent anomalies in measurement could only be solved by introducing some basic notion of a conscious observer. To take the leap of faith required to make the required connection between the external world and our minds, we have to go beyond conventional quantum theories and make new hypotheses that postulate that consciousness influences the actual outcome of perceived events, and does not just observe them.

48 The goat-like figure is usually connected to Chiron who is sometimes referred to as 'the wounded healer.' In Greek mythology Chiron was the most advanced of the centaurs, who were notorious for being uncultured, overly indulgent in sex and drink and given to violence. Chiron, unlike his fellow centaurs, was intelligent, civilized and kind. Although a great healer, he could not heal himself, so he has become associated with traumas and wounds which are incurable, but may be worked with, on their own terms, and transformed into one's greatest strengths. Interestingly, in Chinese iconography, the character for 'difficulty' is the same as for 'opportunity' thus offering the same message. In our modern world where we may 'expect' to be healed and see it as a failure if we are not, such insight is very helpful in moving us towards a more positive and life-affirming position; after all, even death can be seen as an opportunity.

49 Chuang-tzu was a 4th Century BCE Chinese philosopher. He argues that our life is limited whilst the amount of things to know is unlimited, so to think (or pretend) that we might know everything (or even anything!) is foolish. According to Chuang-tzu our most carefully considered conclusions might be misguided as they are dependent upon our limited knowledge, our inability to understand the full workings of our infinitely mysterious universe, and because our reflections of truth are always coloured by our past experiences (which if they were different might lead us to different conclusions.) Chuang-tzu is most famous for Taoist and Zen-like statements and ideas that attempt to 'bend our minds' from a set position, such as in the butterfly dream example.

50 Kabbalah is usually described as the mystical teachings of Judaism but, in our modern world, it has taken on a much wider meaning and is not allied to any particular religion or belief system. We don't know the true origins of Kabbalah but it is certainly many thousands of years old, its longevity perhaps at least partly because it adapts itself to whatever use it is put. Applied to ourselves, Kabbalah is a practical system of self-development based around a diagram known as the Tree of Life, which through its visual structure helps us make connections between apparently unrelated facts that then become gems of meaningful wisdom. Kabbalah aims to help you live life to the full, and learn to be here with respect for the planet itself and all the life forms it supports, and stresses that when we care for our environment, both locally and generally, we are also bringing our deepest, spiritual consciousness to earth.

51 Kabbalists are people who are interested in the teachings of Kabbalah and use at least some aspects of these teachings to inform their understanding about life. Kabbalists do not have to belong to any particular religion and indeed people practicing Kabbalah include atheists as well as Buddhists, Christians, Jews and people from other beliefs.

52 The words 'as above so below' are used in one form or anoth-

er in most esoteric teachings. The concept was first laid out in The Emerald Tablet of Hermes Trismegistus, in the words 'That which is Below corresponds to that which is Above, and that which is Above, corresponds to that which is Below.' Basically this is simply saying that what happens on any level happens on every other level, but it is more often used in the sense of the the individual and the universe, basically asserting our individual identity is a mirror of the universe. The Judaeo-Christian concept that we are 'created in God's image' asserts the same thing. As many myths, particularly ancient ones, include stories of the foibles, limitations and sometimes downright bad behaviour of gods and goddesses, it is sometimes useful to remember that our 'imperfections' do not separate us from our divinity but may just as well be a manifestation of it.

53 Through connecting with our heart and living in a 'heart-centred' way, we learn to transform frustration and anxiety into excitement and joy, and we become more able to experience the qualities of love, freedom, peace and happiness that are at the core of our true nature. To be heart-centred is to live in the present moment, experiencing everything as fresh and new and thus having less stress and anxiety in our lives. We start to say 'yes' to life with whatever experiences it may bring, even the more uncomfortable ones. In Kabbalah, the heart is connected to the qualities of courage and compassion and to live in a heart-full way is the aim of all our inner work. If we face death with heart we centre ourselves on that within us which is truly inviolable, immutable and immortal.

54 The 'source' is often used as a synonym of more limited and emotive words such as 'god' or 'deity' or 'creator'. It is all those things but it is also more if we consider going back far enough to where whatever exists must arise from somewhere. The interesting speculation then is, if there is a source of everything, where does it go after is has been sourced – do we return, as it were, to our source or do we 'go elsewhere'?

55 When Kabbalists look within any particular religion they inevitably find different aspects of that religion will correspond to different areas of the Tree of Life (thus proving the universality of the model.). For instance, it is possible to relate various aspects of the story of Jesus' life to the Tree as when he said 'My Father and I are One' he was uniting the Supernal Triad with the middle triangle of the Tree of Life. United, these two triangles form a hexagram, used by both Jewish people and occultists as a symbol of the greatest spiritual truth. The purpose of relating Jesus' life or that of any other religious leader to the Tree of Life, or of relating different religious ideas to Kabbalah, is primarily that it offers us a greater understanding of our own beliefs and interests. It may also profoundly affect the manifestation of tolerance and understanding between different religious traditions. Christianity has a specifically strong link with Kabbalah, and, indeed, Jesus is sometimes described as the greatest Kabbalist to ever have lived.

56 Elisabeth Kubler-Ross (1926-2004) was a psychiatrist and prolific author whose bestselling book, *On Death and Dying* made her an internationally acclaimed author. This revolutionary book is required reading in many medical, nursing, and psychology courses and whenever the subject of death and dying is discussed her work is almost invariably not only present but of central relevance. I highly recommend a visit to her website at www. elisabethkublerross.com for very moving tributes to her work and many insights into our subject.

57 Existential psychology is based on existential philosophy that was originally based on the writings of the philosophers Kierkegaard and Nietzsche. Existentialism was named and made popular in the 1940s by Jean-Paul Sartre, Albert Camus and others who felt that a focus on self-reliance, authenticity, responsibility, and mortality was the best way forward for human development. This approach to human nature is called 'existential' because it has a focus on existence in the here and now. At each moment, each of us is free to choose

what we will be and do. Our decisions are based not on what we have genetically inherited or how our parents treated us, but how we interpret and respond to the world at each given instant. Conscious choice and responsibility are central to existential psychology, and our behaviour is believed to be primarily based on our anxieties about our existence and an innate desire for freedom.

58 James Bugental is a central theorist and advocate of Existential and Humanistic Therapy. Humanistic Therapy is a method explicitly concerned with the human dimension of psychology and the human context for the development of psychological theory. Bugental's inspiring postulates as quoted here form the basis of the movement that has been extremely influential in the furthering of human understanding since the 1950s, as the names of some of the major characters involved readily indicates: Wilhelm Reich, Abraham Maslow, Carl Rogers, Rollo May, Roberto Assagioli, Martin Buber, Ronnie Laing, Fritz Perls and Erich Fromm. Humanistic psychology looks beyond a medical model of psychology in order to open up a non-pathologising view of an individual, stressing the healthy aspects of a person's life rather than the pathological ones. Self-actualisation (having a strong and healthy sense of self) is a central, if sometimes unspoken, aim of the movement which also stresses that society develops and improves through individual self-actualisation.

59 When we are born we have no sense of self, coming into this world without knowledge or self-consciousness. Gradually through experiences of pleasure and pain, and the development of a memory, we separate from our original sense of being and develop the ego which both protects us during our development but also leads us to lose contact with our essential self. Gradually through our early years changes in our mental processes create a self-image in an attempt to bring coherence to what is happening to us in our day-to-day life experiences. Ego is constantly engaged in organizing and reorganizing everything experienced through our senses to create a unique viewpoint out of the constant stream of

conflicting information that we meet. It is said ego is a good servant but a terrible master; we need to have ego to help us feel unified and to survive the onslaught of all our everyday experiences; the problem is when we forget we have ego for this purpose and we believe our ego is all there is to us, leading us to lose touch with our essential nature.

60 Stoicism is a school of philosophy that arose in Greece in the third century BCE. The core belief of Stoicism is that human freedom is maintained through choosing to be in accord with nature. Stoicism therefore stresses the development of self-control and the strong will as the way to deal with powerful and destructive emotions. Concerned with improving our spiritual well-being, Stoics focus on virtue, reason, and natural law, believing that through mastering our passions and emotions, we find equilibrium in ourselves and bring this equilibrium to the world.

61 Saint Augustine (354-430) was a philosopher and theologian of Berber descent, and is considered to be one of the most important figures in the development of Western Christianity. A deeply spiritual being, he introduced the concepts of original sin and the notion that war can be justified when in the service of the good. His teachings were used by early Christians in their fight for supremacy over other religions and beliefs such as paganism and witchcraft. Despite how his teachings have been used and interpreted in many various (and sometimes conflicting) ways over the centuries, his central doctrine concerned the supremacy of love over all else and one of his most famous (and useful) statements is: 'Love, and do what you will.'

62 Pierre Teilhard de Chardin (1881-1955) was a French Jesuit priest whose primary book, *The Phenomenon of Man*, set forth an expansive and mind-expanding account of the unfolding of the cosmos. As he abandoned traditional interpretations of creation, his ideas were opposed by his church superiors, and his work was denied publication during his lifetime. However John XXIII rehabilitated him posthumously, and,

since then, his works have been considered a major influence on the contemporary church's position on evolution. Teilhard believed in an evolutionary pathway from creation to the development of the noosphere (a term he invented, signifying the sum total of human development) in the present, to a vision of the Omega Point in the future where everyone and everything reaches a state of enlightenment or 'Christ consciousness.' The notion that we can develop and grow without being wholly dependant upon the incarnation of Christ, whilst upsetting many traditionalists and fundamentalists, seems to be clearly born out by our human experience.

63 Albert Camus (1913-1960) was a French author and philosopher who won the Nobel prize in 1957. Although often associated with existentialism, Camus saw himself as a free man and disliked being associated with any particular school of thought, and particularly argued against nihilism, believing that at some future stage of our development we will awaken to our fullest human potential. Camus opposed any kind of fundamentalism, including Fascism and Marxism, and stressed how we experience our world in a dualistic way, through happiness and sadness, dark and light, life and death, and so on. He emphasized that happiness is fleeting and that the human condition is one of mortality, not to be morbid and depressing but to help us gain a greater appreciation for life and happiness. Camus believed we have to value our lives and existence to the fullest even though we know we will eventually die.

64 See note 13 for more about Sartre. To find a meaning in life is central to human existence because when we reflect on our experiences to try and find meaning we are engaging with the core of all our activities.

65 Don Hanlon Johnson is professor of Somatics at the California Institute of Integral Studies (CIIS) in San Francisco. An ex-Jesuit, he has published several books on somatics, stressing the difference between 'body' awareness (what we physically look like from outside) and 'somatic' awareness

(what we physically feel like from inside.) All of his books are highly recommended, perhaps especially *Body: Recovering Our Sensual Wisdom* and *Body and Democracy.* His rather unique style of writing in which he combines deep investigation of his subject with engaging, personal narrative makes the subject come alive, thus matching his intent in shifting your focus from the 'corpse' (the body as object) to the liquid, breathing reality of our inner somatic awareness.

66 The quote continues: 'and yet I say unto you, that Solomon in all his glory was not arrayed like one of these.' In other words, if we stop striving and allow ourselves to to 'just be', to flow with whatever is, then we have nothing to worry about, nothing to be anxious about, and our experience (and fate) will unfold naturally and in line with everything and everyone else.

67 Epictetus (55-135) was a Greek philosopher of the Stoic school. He believed our best aim was to become master of our own lives, but always tempered by compassion and care. A famous story involves him, in his latter years, adopting a friend's child who would otherwise have been left to die. His most famous statements say, in one way or another, that we are not troubled by events but by our perception of and attitude towards them (as is exemplified by the quote given here.)

68 *What We May Be* ('we know what we are but not what we may be') is a quote from William Shakespeare that the psychosynthesis author Piero Ferrucci made the title of his excellent book on personal and spiritual development. It stresses the importance of our potential which is always limitless, even in the last moments of life, for whatever we know of ourselves, or however well we know ourselves, we can never know what we might be, do or become in the future, even in the next moment. I have stressed several times in this book the importance of being aware of our imminent death; the equally important corollary to this is to remember our always imminent and emerging life energy.

69 The 'Zenrin' is a text from Japanese Zen Buddhism, it's full title meaning 'An Anthology of Passages from the Forests of Zen'. A collection of somewhere approaching 5000 quotes it was first assembled in the 15th Century but not published until much later. The quotations it includes come not only from Zen masters and Buddhist scriptures but also from Confucianism and Taoism. The Zenrin was originally compiled as a study aid for Zen monks, but its use in the modern world is no less powerful as the example statements chosen here show. A useful selection of excerpts can be found in Paul Reps seminal work *Zen Flesh, Zen Bones*. It might change from moment to moment, but one of my abiding favourite quotes is 'Tread so softly so not to touch the grass.'

70 Karl Marx, Eric Morecombe and Frank Sinatra are too well-known to need comment beyond pointing out the abiding value of humour when faced with difficult transitions.

✳

Bibliography

Psychosynthesis *Roberto Assagioli* Turnstone, UK, 1975
The Phenomenon of Man *Teilhard de Chardin* Harper, UK, 1976
The Book of Chuang-Tzu *Chuang Tzu* Penguin, UK, 2006
Awakening Osiris *Normandi Ellis* Phanes Press, US, 1988
What We May be *Piero Ferrucci* Turnstone, UK, 1982
The Prophet *Kahlil Gibran* Pan, UK, 1991
The Dead Good Funerals Book *Gill and Fox* E of I, UK, 1996
Touching Peace *Thich Nhat Hanh* Parallex, UK, 1993
Somatics *Thomas Hanna* Da Capo, US, 1988
Body, Spirit and Democracy *Don H. Johnson* North Atlantic, US, 1994
Living Your Dying *Stanley Keleman* Random House, US, 1977
On Death and Dying *Elizabeth Kubler-Ross* Collier, US, 1970
Design For Dying *Timothy Leary* Harper, US, 1997
Who Dies? *Stephen Levine* Gateway, UK, 2000
Andrew Marvell Complete Poetry *ed. de F Lord* Dent, UK, 1984
Kabbalah for Life *Will Parfitt* Rider, UK, 2006
Gestalt Therapy *Perls, Hefferline and Goodman* Penguin, UK, 1973
Zen Flesh Zen Bones *Paul Reps* Arkana, UK, 1991
Email to the Universe *Robert A Wilson* New Falcon, US, 2005

(many of these books have more recent editions available,
see Amazon for details of availability.)

✳

About the Author

Will Parfitt has worked in the fields of personal and spiritual development for over thirty years. He trained in psychosynthesis and is a registered psychotherapist, leading courses in England and Europe. He also has a private practice in Glastonbury, England, where he lives, offering psychotherapy, mentoring, coaching, supervision and spiritual guidance. He is the author of several books, titles of which are at the front of this book.

You can find more information on Will and his current work at his website:

www.willparfitt.com

✳

Index

�ֹ

PS AVALON PUBLISHING

About PS Avalon

PS Avalon Publishing is an independent and committed publisher offering a complete publishing service, including editorial, manuscript preparation, printing, promotion, marketing and distribution. As a small publisher enabled to take full advantage of the latest technological advances, PS Avalon Publishing can offer an alternative route for aspiring authors working in our particular fields of interest.

As well as publishing, we offer a comprehensive education programme including courses, seminars, group retreats, and other opportunities for personal and spiritual growth. Whilst the nature of our work means we engage with people from all around the world, we are based in Glastonbury which is in the West Country of England.

new poetry books

Our purpose is to bring you the best new poetry with a psychospiritual content. Our intent is to make poetry relevant again, offering work that is contemplative and inspirational, with a dark, challenging edge.

self development books

We publish inspiring reading material aimed at enhancing your life development without overburdening you with too many words. Everything is kept as simple and as accessible as possible.

journals

With its full colour design, easy on-line availability, and most of all with its exciting and inspiring contents, The Synthesist journal is a popular offering to the psychospiritual world and beyond.

PS AVALON PUBLISHING
Box 1865, Glastonbury,
Somerset BA6 8YR, U.K.

www.psavalon.com

info@psavalon.com

Printed in the United Kingdom
by Lightning Source UK Ltd.
126563UK00001B/148/A